Emily Jane Brontë.　 　 Transcribed February 1844

Gondal Poems

A.G.A. ——————— March 6th 1837

There shines the moon, at noon of night.
Vision of Glory - Dream of light !

Holy as heaven - undimmed and pure,
Looking down on the lonely moor -
And lonlier still beneath her ray
That drear moor stretches far away

Till it seems strange that aught can lie
Beyond its zone of silvery sky .

Bright moon - dear moon! when years have past
My weary feet return at last -
And still upon Lake Elnor's breast
Thy solemn rays serenely rest
And still on Elderno's sighing wave
Like moonows over Elbü grave
And Earth's the same but Oh to see
How wildly Time has altered me!
Am I the same being what long ago
Sat watching by that water side
The light of life expiring slow
From his fair cheek and brow of pride ?
Not oft these mountains feel the shine
Of such - Ay - as towering then,
cast from its front of god like divine
A last smile on the heathery plain
And kissed the far off peaks of snow
That gleaming on the horizon shine
As if in summer's warmest glow
Stern winter claimed a loftier throne -
And there he lay among the bloom
His red blood dyed a deeper hue
Shuddering to feel the ghostly gloom
That coming Death around him threw -

THE COMPLETE POEMS

of

Emily Jane Brontë

EDITED FROM THE MANUSCRIPTS
By C. W. HATFIELD

New York

COLUMBIA UNIVERSITY PRESS

ISBN 0-231-01222-5
ISBN 0-231-10347-6 (pbk.)

Published in Great Britain, India, and Pakistan
by the Oxford University Press
London, Bombay, and Karachi

*Clothbound editions of Columbia University Press books
are printed on permanent and durable acid-free paper.*

PRINTED IN THE UNITED STATES OF AMERICA
C 15
P 10 9 8 7 6 5 4

To the Memory of

HENRY HOUSTON BONNELL

CONTENTS

The letters and figures in the first column indicate the sources from which the text of the poems has been derived (see pp. 24–26). If two or more successive poems have the same source, the source is indicated beside the first. Lines printed in italics indicate subsidiary versions of poems from which only variant lines and/or headings are printed. Lines within square brackets indicate incomplete manuscripts from which the first lines of the poems are missing. Figures within parentheses indicate the number of lines in each poem or poetical fragment.

CONTENTS

CONTENTS

CONTENTS

CONTENTS

CONTENTS

ÆT. 21

CONTENTS

ÆT. 22

CONTENTS

CONTENTS

CONTENTS

CONTENTS

CONTENTS

ÆT. 27

ÆT. 28

ÆT. 29

FACSIMILES REPRODUCED IN
THIS VOLUME

The letters and figures in the first column indicate the manuscript. The numbers in the second column indicate poem numbers in this edition.

The first of the two dates on this poem show that it was begun in the Pensionnat Heger and finished at Haworth.

First page of the long narrative poem from which Emily took the section first published as "The Prisoner. A Fragment" in *Poems by Currer, Ellis, and Acton Bell*. Charlotte in 1850 used the first three stanzas with, presumably, two of her own to make the poem published under Emily's name as "The Visionary."

FOREWORD

Irene Tayler

In the maze of error and misappropriation that characterized much early publication of Brontë material, C. W. Hatfield's edition of *The Complete Poems of Emily Jane Brontë* stood out as a model of tactful and rigorous scholarship. It remains the seminal edition to which all others are indebted. Brontë scholars are fortunate to have it available in paperback at last.

Emily Brontë's was a powerful voice in nineteenth-century English poetry, though she is not widely heard now. We are far from certain that she even wanted to be heard. Indeed, a passionate privacy, a stubborn preference for what she called the "world within" as opposed to the "world without," marks all of the small canon left us by this remarkable writer. One novel, a hundred-and-some poems and poetic fragments, and a few scattered private notes and letters make up the body of her extant work. Her vivid accounts of mystical or visionary events suggest that she herself found such experience an anchor in "the world's storm-troubled sphere." Certainly she had a dark view of "the world without," and this view seems to have blackened all the more when she finally, reluctantly, addressed that world. This first happened in 1846, when she allowed her sister Charlotte to publish twenty-one of her poems in a collection of poems by the three sisters, Emily, Charlotte, and Anne. Then, as if in violent reaction, she wrote *Wuthering Heights* in a matter of months, having it ready for readers by July 1846. After these two forays into the outer world, she seems to have virtually stopped writing.

Emily Brontë was thirty when she died, on December 19, 1848. She had been writing poetry since at least as early as her teens, much of it revolving around the imaginary world of "Gondal" conceived in 1831 by her and her closest companion, the quiet youngest sister, Anne; this fantastical land occupied much of Emily's creative attention for the rest of her life. Of her surviving poems and fragments, many more than half are spoken by Gondal characters or touch on their stories.

But not all her poetry concerned Gondal. In February 1844, when she was twenty-five, Emily went back over all her earlier poems and transcribed a selection of them into two notebooks. The only surviving new poems written after this date appear in one or the other of those notebooks. (These are labeled "A" and "B" in Hatfield's list of the holograph manuscripts—see page 24.) The manuscript that Hatfield calls "ms B" contains forty-five "Gondal Poems." The other manuscript is headed simply "E.J.B. Transcribed February, 1844," and contains thirty-one poems that have no Gondal references and often reflect intensely personal experience. Although she did not transcribe her poems in the order in which they had been written, she did note the original dates on which they had been composed or completed, so that we may reconstruct with some confidence the process of her poetic development.

One important development, not generally observed by Brontë scholars, is that this retrospection of 1844 not only ushered in the period of Emily's greatest poetic achievement but also marked another, perhaps related, turning point in her work: a burgeoning of poems that concern mystical or visionary happenings. Certainly the Gondal poems continue after this point, including one that many consider her best: "Cold in the earth" (No. 182). But among the non-Gondal poems written during or after February 1844 are Emily's most powerful and revealing expressions of her spiritual life (see, for example, Nos. 168, 170, 174, 176, 181, 183, 184, 188, and 191).

Then in the autumn of 1845 Charlotte discovered Emily's notebooks and read them. Charlotte's later public account of this climactic moment, and of Emily's resistance to publication, is quoted at the beginning of Hatfield's introduction. But in Charlotte's personal letters we get a much sharper sense of the cost to Emily of her sister's intrusion into what had previously been profoundly private work. As Charlotte lamented to a friend, once she had "wrung out" of Emily her "reluctant consent to have the 'rhymes' as they were contemptuously termed, published," Emily simply stopped referring to them—or referred to them only "with scorn." After this Emily wrote only two more poems and her novel. Although she lived another two and a half years after finishing *Wuthering Heights*, she seems increasingly to have cut her ties to "the world without."

Of the two poems that she did write, the one from the personal notebook—"No coward soul is mine" (No. 191)—was written while she was composing her novel and is widely thought to reflect certain of the novel's themes. The other (No. 192) is scrawled nearly illegibly in the Gondal notebook and dated September 1846, after she had finished *Wuthering Heights*. It is a long, rambling poetic fragment spoken by an unnamed Gondal character who has left home and is fighting in a brutal foreign war that means nothing to him. More than a year and a half later, just months before her death, Emily returned to this fragment and reduced it to its bitter core, a scathing judgment on "our own humanity" (No. 193).

Emily Brontë's chosen companion, the quiet Anne, died a few months after Emily did, leaving of the original six young Brontës only Charlotte to struggle with Emily's literary remains and serve as her interpreter. Charlotte did her best to adjust her most brilliant but difficult and heterodox sister's reputation, to make it accord with what she herself considered acceptable norms. She republished *Wuthering Heights* with a rather apologetic preface; rewrote poetic lines (as in No. 191); added lines of her own (see No. 190); and may even have attributed a poem of her own to Emily (see pages 255–56). But if Charlotte altered Emily's work, certainly Emily altered Charlotte's. Grieving, shaken by loneliness, and in crisis as a writer, Charlotte immersed herself in Emily's literary remains and found in them a vision that empowered her own last and greatest novel, *Villette*.

Other creative women, too, may find Emily Brontë's vision

empowering. Ironically, her very reluctance to publish makes an important point. Writing within a culture that finds or assumes that women especially value community, cooperation, family relationship, and an "ethic of caring," Emily speaks emphatically for the values of solitude, defiance, and liberty. The "Comforter" or "God of Visions," whom she invoked as her own compelling male version of the traditionally female muse and who survives in a much distorted form as Heathcliff in her novel, embodies Emily's experience of the woman artist's need to be fierce and isolated at times, to turn sternly away from the world of social and affectional ties, to scorn the posture of compromise even when she must assume it. I think that what Charlotte experienced as "a certain harshness" in Emily's "powerful and peculiar character" was for Emily herself a breath of life and source of art—one function of her visionary "world within."

Hatfield's respectful and uncluttered edition contains most of the tools readers will need to hear this strong poetic voice for themselves. However suspicious Emily Brontë may have been of the "world without," our present fast-rising interest in women poets of the nineteenth century means that her voice will now be increasingly heard, and her vision attended.

PREFACE

Among those who have assisted me in my search for manuscripts or who have furnished me with photographs or photostatic
copies of manuscripts are the Trustees of the Brontë Parsonage
Museum; Mrs C. M. Edgerley, the Honorary Secretary of the
Brontë Society; Mrs Henry H. Bonnell; Miss Fannie E. Ratchford; Mr William T. H. Howe; the Trustees of the Henry E.
Huntington Library and Art Gallery; Miss Helen Brown; and
Mr Davidson Cook. I am glad to be able to record here my cordial
thanks to all of them.

C. W. HATFIELD

April 23, 1941

INTRODUCTORY

INTRODUCTION

In the "Biographical Notice of Ellis and Acton Bell," printed in the 1850 edition of *Wuthering Heights and Agnes Grey,* Charlotte Brontë says:

About five years ago, my two sisters and myself, after a somewhat prolonged period of separation, found ourselves re-united and at home. Resident in a remote district, where education had made little progress, and where, consequently, there was no inducement to seek social intercourse beyond our own domestic circle, we were wholly dependent on ourselves and each other, on books and study, for the enjoyments and occupations of life. The highest stimulus, as well as the liveliest pleasures we had known from childhood upwards, lay in attempts at literary composition; formerly we used to show each other what we wrote, but of late years this habit of communication and consultation had been discontinued; hence it ensued, that we were mutually ignorant of the progress we might respectively have made.

One day, in the autumn of 1845, I accidentally lighted on a MS. volume of verse in my sister Emily's handwriting. Of course, I was not surprised, knowing that she could and did write verse: I looked it over, and something more than surprise seized me—a deep conviction that these were not common effusions, nor at all like the poetry women generally write. I thought them condensed and terse, vigorous and genuine. To my ear they had also a peculiar music—wild, melancholy and elevating.

My sister Emily was not a person of demonstrative character, nor one on the recesses of whose mind and feelings even those nearest and dearest to her could, with impunity, intrude unlicensed; it took hours to reconcile her to the discovery I had made, and days to persuade her that such poems merited publication. I knew, however, that a mind like hers could not be without some latent spark of honourable ambition, and refused to be discouraged in my attempts to fan that spark to flame. . . . We agreed to arrange a small selection of our poems. . . . We veiled our names under those of Currer, Ellis, and Acton

Bell; the ambiguous choice being dictated by a sort of conscientious scruple at assuming Christian names positively masculine, while we did not like to declare ourselves women, because we had a vague impression that authoresses were liable to be looked on with prejudice. . . .

The little book *Poems by Currer, Ellis, and Acton Bell* (London: Aylott and Jones) was published on May 2, 1846. It contains 21 poems by Emily Jane Brontë, her pseudonym "Ellis" being printed at the end of each poem.

The 21 poems were selected from two manuscript books which had been commenced as transcript books for her finished poems in February, 1844. One of them was headed with the inscription "Gondal Poems," Gondal being the name of a fictitious island, about which she and her younger sister, Anne, had been writing stories and poetry almost from childhood. The other manuscript book was used for her finished poems which apparently did not relate to Gondal; and this was doubtless the manuscript book which her sister Charlotte found and read on that momentous day in the autumn of 1845.

It has been thought not improbable that Charlotte selected and "edited" Emily's poems for printing in the volume of 1846, as she did, after Emily's death, for the volume of 1850 (see under "G" and "H," pp. 25, 26). But there are alterations and additions in the manuscripts in Emily's handwriting, which seem to show that she at least assisted in the selection and titling of the poems. However that may be, in the present volume precedence is given to the *manuscript* versions of the poems, and the differences and additions found in the volume of 1846 are shown under the index letter "G," below the manuscript text.

In 1850, Charlotte Brontë's publisher expressed a desire to publish, with a new edition of *Wuthering Heights and Agnes Grey,* a selection from the literary remains of Ellis and Acton Bell. From the two transcript books of poems by Emily, 17 poems not previously printed were selected. On this occasion there is no doubt that Charlotte Brontë "edited" the poems, as will be seen by comparing the manuscript versions (printed herein under the index letters "A" and "B") with the altered lines given under index letter "H." Not only did she make numerous alterations, but she added titles and verses to some of the poems. Altogether, she included 18 poems in her "Selections from Poems by Ellis Bell," but only 17 of them have been found in Emily's manuscripts. The poem for which there does not appear to be any manuscript authority is printed on p. 255 of this book, with the question, "Who was the author of this poem?" Maybe the answer is Charlotte's secret. Did she write it herself, with the hope that in an "autobiographical" form, and among her sister's poems, it would help towards a better understanding of Emily? The poem seems to express what might well be Charlotte's thoughts about her sister, but (in the first three verses) not what Emily would write about herself.

In 1854, Charlotte Brontë married her father's curate, the Reverend Arthur Bell Nicholls. She died in 1855.

In May, 1860, the poem "A Farewell to Alexandria" (No. 108) was printed in *The Cornhill Magazine,* presumably from a book containing transcripts of 34 poems by Emily Jane Brontë, all in the handwriting of the Reverend A. B. Nicholls, for the errors made by Mr Nicholls in transcribing are in the printed copy. A new title, "The Outcast Mother," was substituted in *The Cornhill Magazine.*

In 1861, Mr Brontë died, and Mr Nicholls returned to his early home at Banagher, Ireland, taking with him all the manuscripts of Emily Jane Brontë which had not been destroyed, as well as those of her sisters Charlotte and Anne (died 1849) and her brother Patrick Branwell Brontë (died 1848).

The poems which had been published continued to be printed, but nothing further was added to them until many years afterwards. In 1895, Mr Clement King Shorter visited Mr Nicholls and purchased from him on behalf of a friend (Mr Thomas James Wise) a large quantity of manuscripts, including every poems manuscript of Emily Jane Brontë which is known to exist, except the "Gondal Poems" manuscript which is now in the British Museum.

Almost all of the poems manuscripts were in minute script (print style); and the similarity of the writing of each of the four Brontë children seems to have caused Mr Wise to make a number of errors in deciding who wrote the manuscripts which bore no signature or initials. In preparing them for binding into small books, some of Charlotte's and Branwell's and Anne's were allocated to Emily, and so we find Emily's name on the binding of unsigned poems which are in the handwriting of her sisters and brother.

Mr Wise parted with most of these small manuscript books, but before he did so their contents were copied and the transcripts were given to Mr Shorter.

In *Charlotte Brontë and Her Circle,* published by Hodder and Stoughton in 1896, Mr Shorter gave one unpublished poem by Emily Jane Brontë (No. 63; B11); and in his "Relics of Emily Brontë," printed in *The Woman at Home,* August, 1897, he gave another (No. 133; B17).

Five years later, an important addition was made to the poetry of Emily Jane Brontë by the publication, in an edition limited to 110 copies, of *Poems by Charlotte, Emily, and Anne Brontë Now for the First Time Printed* (New York: Dodd, Mead and Company, 1902). The book contained 67 poems by Emily, which it was not quite correct to say were "for the first time printed," for two of the poems were those printed in 1896 and 1897 respectively. The book contains the following statement:

The poems have been deciphered with some difficulty from *the original manuscripts* . . . some [34] of Emily's are written in an ordinary, quite legible handwriting, and are signed and dated . . . a few [33 poems] of Emily's verses which are here printed are written on little scraps of paper of various sizes, in minute angular characters, almost illegible, without punctuation, and the spelling often at fault. . . . Some of Emily's are signed or initialed and dated at the top. With others, only the date is given.

The first "complete edition" of Emily Jane Brontë's poems was published in 1910. This was the first volume of *The Complete Works of Emily Brontë.* In two volumes; Vol. I: *Poetry.* Edited by Clement Shorter (London: Hodder and Stoughton). In this volume Mr Shorter included all the poems which had been published in 1846, 1850, and 1902, and 71 poems which had "never before been printed."

In 1915, a volume of poems was published which contained two previously unpublished poems by Emily Jane Brontë (part of No. 192 and the whole of No. 193): *Brontë Poems: Selections from the*

Poetry of Charlotte, Emily, Anne, and Branwell Brontë. Edited, with an Introduction, by Arthur C. Benson (London: Smith, Elder & Co., 15 Waterloo Place). Most of the errors made in the volume of 1910 are to be found in this volume.

Mr Shorter was dissatisfied with his book, and about the year 1919 he expressed a wish that I would prepare a volume of the poems. He sent me the transcripts of the poems which had been made from the original manuscripts, and along with them came a copy of the poems volume printed in 1910, which I then saw for the first time. It soon became clear to me that the 71 poems first printed in that volume were not all written by Emily Jane Brontë. Many were related to the early prose stories of Charlotte and Branwell; one had been printed as Charlotte's in 1902, and four had been printed as Anne's since 1850. I decided that not less than 25 of the poems would have to be omitted from the book I was to prepare. The transcripts furnished me with many new and obviously more correct readings of the text of the poems than had appeared in the volume of 1902, and upon which Mr Shorter seems to have relied for a large part of his volume of 1910.

In the course of my search for original manuscripts I heard of the unique collection of Brontëana which had been acquired by Mr H. H. Bonnell of Philadelphia. In reply to my enquiry about manuscripts, Mr Bonnell very generously sent me a typed catalogue containing full details of his Brontë treasures. Therein, I found described among the manuscripts of Emily Jane Brontë most of the poems printed in Mr Shorter's volume which I considered were not written by her. I gave Mr Bonnell a list of the poems and described to him the individual characteristics which he would find in the writing of each manuscript (if in print style) provided that my surmises as to authorship were correct. Mr Bonnell confirmed my suspicions in every case. The covers in which the manuscripts were bound had the name "Emily Brontë" printed on them. Bound within one of the covers were 59 poems or poetical fragments by Emily, two poems by Charlotte, and two by Branwell; in another, one poem by Emily, and four poems and one prose fragment by Branwell; in another, five poems by Anne and none by Emily;

and in another, five by Branwell and none by Emily. Altogether, Mr Bonnell had the manuscripts of twenty of the poems which had been wrongly attributed to "Emily Brontë."

The volume which I prepared was published in 1923: *The Complete Poems of Emily Jane Brontë*. Edited by Clement Shorter. Arranged and collated, with Bibliography and Notes, by C. W. Hatfield (Hodder and Stoughton, Ltd., London).

The exclusion of so many poems which had been printed in 1910 and 1915 and accepted as genuine caused surprise and doubt in the minds of some reviewers at the time, but my evidence was sufficient, and none of the excluded poems has ever again been printed as the work of Emily Jane Brontë. The chronological arrangement of the poems with known dates, then attempted for the first time, was appreciated by many readers; and I have, therefore, in the present volume, attempted to arrange *all* of the poems in chronological order. Many other dates have been furnished by the manuscripts which have become available for examination since the volume of 1923 was published, but there are still several poems which cannot be dated, and the placing of these must be considered as conjectural. Where poems or poetical studies appear on a separate leaf and only one of the items is dated, the whole of the items in the manuscript are printed with the dated poem.

I was soon made aware that the volume of the poems printed in 1923 was neither so complete nor so textually accurate as I had believed. In 1926 I was informed by Mr Davidson Cook, the authority on the life and poetry of Burns and on Scottish songs generally, that in the course of his research work he had come across a manuscript volume of poems by Emily Jane Brontë in the library of Sir A. J. Law at Honresfeld in Lancashire. This was the manuscript which is indexed "A" in the present volume. It carries the bookplate of Thomas James Wise, and is stamped: "Bound by Rivière and Son for T. J. Wise." On the flyleaf is autographed in pencil: "William Law, Littleborough, nr. Manchester. February 5th, 1897."

All of the poems in this manuscript had been printed, 15 in 1846, 8 in 1850, and the remainder in the limited edition of 1902; but comparisons with the manuscript show many differences in the text of the poems. A large number of alterations I identified as in the handwriting of Charlotte Brontë, when Mr Cook sent me photographs of some of the manuscript pages. Mr Cook's remarks on this manuscript ("Emily Brontë's Poems: Some Textual Corrections and Unpublished Verses," which appeared in the August, 1926, number of *The Nineteenth Century and After*) made clear the need for a new volume of the poems, and I commenced a search for other manuscripts which has continued until the present time.

On learning that I proposed to prepare another volume of the poems of Emily Jane Brontë, Mr Bonnell took his collection of her manuscripts to a photographer, so that I could be furnished with photographs; but he did not live to send them to me. It was from Mrs Bonnell that I received them—beautifully clear copies—and with them came the sad news that Mr Bonnell had died suddenly on November 7, 1926—only two days after he had written to me: "The E.B. poems I shall have photographed at once."

Mr A. B. Nicholls had died on December 13, 1906, and I learned in the course of my enquiries that many Brontë treasures which he had kept for nearly fifty years had been sold at auction by Sotheby, Wilkinson and Hodge, London, on July 26, 1907, among them being a manuscript book of poems by Emily Jane Brontë. This was the "Gondal Poems" manuscript, which is indexed "B" in the present volume. It was purchased by Mrs George Murray Smith, the widow of Charlotte Brontë's publisher. At the time of my enquiry, the business of Smith, Elder and Company (George Murray Smith) had been incorporated with the firm of John Murray, but a letter from me brought a courteous reply from Sir John Murray that the manuscript was in the possession of the son of the late Mr George Murray Smith. My letter to Mr Smith's son brought a distinct refusal to allow the manuscript to be examined; and I was informed that all similar requests met with a refusal. A few years ago, the manuscript was bequeathed to the Trustees of the British Museum, and it became available for examination.

Many small scraps of paper containing rough drafts of poems by Emily Jane Brontë had been received by Mr Wise from Mr Nicholls in 1895. I learned that a number of these had become the property of Mr H. Buxton Forman, whose collection of Brontë manuscripts was sold at the Anderson Galleries in New York in March, 1920.

A kind correspondent in America made enquiries and informed me that the Emily Jane Brontë manuscripts had been purchased by Mr Harry B. Smith of New York. Mr Smith declined to give any information about the manuscripts; he said that he intended to use them with other material for a book he was writing. A year or two later I heard that some of the manuscripts were offered for sale, and soon afterwards that they had been purchased by Mr William T. H. Howe of New York and Cincinnati. Mr Howe very generously sent me photostatic copies of the manuscripts which he had obtained: 33 poems or parts of poems by Emily, and the remaining 5 of the poems which Mr Shorter had printed as Emily's, 3 of which were in the handwriting of Charlotte, and 2 in that of Branwell.

Two of the poems in the Harry B. Smith collection did not go to Mr Howe. They were purchased for the library of Texas University, and Miss Fannie E. Ratchford, the librarian in charge of the special collections there, kindly furnished me with photostatic copies.

For some years, Miss Ratchford had been on the lookout for the manuscript "written in an ordinary, quite legible handwriting," which had been used for 34 of the poems in the volume of 1902; and in September, 1931, she located it in the Henry E. Huntington Library at San Marino. It was described as follows:

Emily Brontë   Holo MS.91pp.8vo.
Collection of Manuscript Poems.   1835–1845. Haworth. HM2581.

Miss Ratchford obtained a photostatic page of the manuscript, but did not recognise the writing as that of Emily Jane Brontë, and she sent the photostat to me. The writing was that of Mr Nicholls. The Trustees of the Henry E. Huntington Library very kindly allowed me to have the use of a complete photostatic copy of the manuscript.

All of the 34 poems had been copied from the manuscripts indexed "A" and "B" in the present volume. They reveal that 34 of the poems "now printed for the first time" in 1902 were *not* printed from the original manuscripts.

After the death of Mr Nicholls's second wife, there was sold by auction in London on June 19, 1914, a "note-book" containing copies of poems by the Brontë sisters, all in the handwriting of Mr Nicholls. Therein, arranged in chronological order, are the 34 poems which are in the Huntington Library manuscript, but with differences in the text, and with titles to some of the poems. The two manuscripts are the source of many of the inaccuracies printed in previous volumes of the poems of Emily Jane Brontë. The "notebook" of Mr Nicholls is now in the collection of Mrs H. H. Bonnell.

The manuscripts of 14 minor poems or poetical fragments, which were first printed in 1910, have not been located, and I am, therefore, relying on the transcripts, made from the original manuscripts and given to me more than twenty years ago by Mr Shorter, for the text printed herein. There may be a few errors of transcription in them, but if so it is unlikely that they are of any importance. The poems are those which are indexed "J," the letter being followed by figures indicating the page on which each poem was printed in the volume of 1910.

The lines of Emily Jane Brontë's poems are rarely indented in her manuscripts. In the present volume, the manuscript arrangement of the lines is followed in preference to the customary pairing of rhymed lines by indention.

One interesting aspect of the poems is that they identify the mind of the writer with the author of that powerful story *Wuthering Heights,* which some ill-informed writers have attempted to attribute to the author's sister Charlotte or her brother Branwell. Mr Charles Morgan, in his admirable essay on "Emily Brontë," [1] points out that

Emily's genius is plainly dominant in "Wuthering Heights," unless we are to assume that the manuscripts of the poems are fraudulent; for whoever wrote the poems wrote "Wuthering Heights," the same unreality of this world, the same greater reality of another, being in them both, and in nothing else that the human mind has produced. The poems and the novel are twins of a unique imagination.

At twenty-two, Emily wrote (No. 146):

> And if I pray, the only prayer
> That moves my lips for me

---

[1] In *The Great Victorians* (London: Ivor Nicholson and Watson), pp. 63–79.

Is—"Leave the heart that now I bear
And give me liberty."

.   .   .   .

'Tis all that I implore—
Through life and death, a chainless soul
With courage to endure! [1]

and the same voice is heard in *Wuthering Heights,* written five
years later, when the elder Cathy is ill—

And the thing that irks me most is this shattered prison after all. I'm
tired of being enclosed here. I'm wearying to escape into that glorious
world and to be always there, not seeing it dimly through tears and
yearning for it through the walls of an aching heart, but really with it
and in it. . . . I shall be incomparably beyond and above you all.

"My sister Emily loved the moors," wrote Charlotte Brontë.
"Flowers brighter than the rose bloomed in the blackest of the
heath for her; out of a sullen hollow in a livid hillside her mind
could make an Eden. She found in the bleak solitude many and
dear delights, and not the least and best loved was—liberty."

In one of her poems she shows a greater love for Earth than for
Heaven (No. 149):

We would not leave our native home
For *any* world beyond the Tomb.
No—rather on thy kindly breast
Let us be laid in lasting rest;
Or waken but to share with thee
A mutual immortality.

And a few years later, in *Wuthering Heights,* again through the
medium of Cathy, she says:

I dreamt once that I was [in Heaven]. Heaven did not seem to be my
home; and I broke my heart with weeping to come back to earth; and
the angels were so angry that they flung me out into the middle of the
heath on the top of Wuthering Heights, where I woke sobbing for joy.

---

[1] "With courage to endure"—This is the line which is carved in the stone
which was fixed in 1939 in the wall, near Shakespeare's monument, in the Poets'
Corner of Westminster Abbey, to the Memory of Charlotte, Emily Jane, and Anne
Brontë.

Of late years there has been increasing interest in the poems relating to Gondal. When the "Gondal Poems" manuscript became available for examination at the British Museum it was seen that many of the poems which had been considered to be of a personal character (owing to Gondal references having been deleted or altered before the poems were printed) were apparently poems of the imagination—part of the Gondal epic which absorbed the minds of Emily and Anne during many years. The reconstruction of the story, in outline at least, is being attempted by Miss Fannie E. Ratchford, probably the most thoroughly equipped student of the Brontë writings. Her explorations in the childhood writings of the Brontës are incorporated in a book entitled *The Brontës' Web of Childhood*. I have been honoured by having a preface concerning "The Gondal Story" incorporated in the present volume.

C. W. HATFIELD

THE GONDAL STORY

by Fannie E. Ratchford

A study of Emily Brontë's poems as they are presented by Mr Hatfield in the present volume reveals that the majority, perhaps all of them, pertain to an imaginative country called Gondal, which she created when she was thirteen or fourteen years old and continued to develop so long as she lived.

When Charlotte, eldest of the four Brontë children and leader in their childish plays, went away to school at Roe Head early in 1831, Emily, refusing to accept her brother Branwell as Charlotte's successor, began a play of her own with her younger sister Anne. Its setting was Gondal, an island in the North Pacific, a land of lakes and mountains and rocky shorelines, with a climate much like Emily's native Yorkshire. Its people were a strong, passionate, freedom-loving race, highly imaginative and intensely patriotic. Politically, Gondal was a confederacy of provinces or kingdoms, each governed by an hereditary ruling family. Between the House of Brenzaida, in the kingdom of Angora, and the House of Exina existed a deadly rivalry which gave direction to the developing play.

When the hardy, far-ranging Gondalan mariners discovered Gaaldine, a large tropical island in the South Pacific, princes of these two families were foremost among the adventurers who explored, conquered, and partitioned it into the kingdoms and provinces of Alexandria, Almedore, Elseraden, Ula, Zalona, and Zedora. Old rivalries and hates went with them, and a goodly number of Emily's poems have to do with the wars of conquest waged by Julius of Brenzaida, King of Almedore, against his Exina neighbors in Zalona.

Emily's and Anne's extensive prose literature of Gondal, constituting a full and detailed background for their somewhat cryptic poems, has been lost, and their verse now stands alone, scantily supplemented by a short journal fragment signed by both girls when they were about fifteen and sixteen; the notes they exchanged on Emily's birthday in 1841 and 1845; and Anne's lists of Gondalan place names and personal names. The poems which Mr Hatfield here gives to the public for the first time complete and as Emily wrote them, were composed through a period of twelve years, from July 12, 1836, the summer following her disastrous Roe Head venture, to May 13, 1848, only six months before her death. Lack of agreement between chronology of composition and story sequence shows that they were not written as progressive plot incidents, but were merely the poetic expression of scenes, dramas, and emotions, long familiar to her inner vision, carried over, no doubt, from her prose creations.

In arranging them in their natural order as an epic we have three guides: Emily's original headings of the poems, now for the first time included; place names and personal names within the poems, here restored in the corrected text; plot connections; and emotional themes. All these, though helpful, are disappointingly inadequate. Only a small per cent of the poems carry headings, and the few headings we have are made up of initials which raise as many perplexing problems as they solve. Varying sets of initials appear for the same character, corresponding to given name, family name, and titles. For example, the heroine of the epic enjoys six certain designations, probably more: Augusta Geraldine Almeda, A.G.A., Rosina of Alcona, A.S., "Sidonia's deity," and Gondal's Queen. Julius Brenzaida, Prince of Angora, King of Almedore, and Emperor of Gondal, is known by all his titles and their abbreviations. Worse still, several characters in the Gondal drama have the same initials, while family names are applied to all of the blood. A.S. stand in one place for Alexander S., Lord of Elbë; in another for Lord Alfred S. of Aspin Castle; again for Lord Alfred's daughter Angelica; and still again for A.G.A. when she was the wife of Lord Alfred. G.S. in one poem is a boy, in another, a woman. The family names Exina and Gleneden appear both with and without distinguishing first initials for the several members of these families. The climax of puzzlement is reached in a poem representing a conversation between a girl named Iërne and her father, headed "I.M. to I.G." Yet this is hardly worse than the heading of two other poems following directly one after the other: "F. De Samara to A.G.A. Written in the Gaaldine Prison Caves," and "F. De Samara to A.G.A." In the first instance, the speaker is clearly a youth named Fernando, who appears in other poems. In the second, he is as certainly Lord Alfred of Aspin Castle. It would seem that Emily made a mistake in copying the second heading.

Place names and personal names are rare, and narrative poems few, while lyrics for the most part yield little definite information. Action shifts back and forth between Gondal and Gaaldine with bewildering rapidity. The long period through which the epic grew makes occasional inconsistencies and even contradictions inevitable. Yet, despite these several difficulties, approximately one-half of the one hundred and ninety-three poems and fragments printed by Mr Hatfield, including the longer and more important pieces, take their places in the Gondal pattern.

Thus Emily Brontë's own voice turns into nonsense the hundreds of pages of Brontë biography based on the subjective interpretation of her poems. At the same time, in the poem beginning, "O thy bright eyes must answer now," she speaks in her own person, proclaiming clearly and emphatically her credo of life, the noblest apology for genius in the language.

The following outline of the reconstructed epic of Gondal, incomplete as it is, and liable to error where gaps in the documents have to be bridged by inference, is submitted to Brontë lovers for their greater understanding and enjoyment of Emily's poems, and to Brontë students for criticism and suggestions.

EMILY BRONTË'S POEMS ARRANGED
AS AN EPIC OF GONDAL

by Fannie E. Ratchford

I. Birth and childhood of A[ugusta] G[eraldine] A[lmeda]

A girl child is born under the planet Venus; what will be the course of her life? Nos. 1 and 2.

Her early years are happy. No. 3.

Sudden misfortune clouds her life. Nos. 4, 8, 109, and 115.

Love dawns. No. 23.

II. A.G.A. and Alexander, Lord of Elbë

Alexander, Lord of Elbë, in Gaaldine, wounded in battle, dies on the shore of Lake Elnor in Gondal, his head pillowed on Augusta's lap. Nos. 17, 18, 19, 21, 78, and 89.

Augusta, returned after many years to the scene of Elbë's death, tells the story of his passing. Nos. 9 and 180.

Augusta is taken prisoner immediately after Elbë's death, and is cast into a dungeon. Nos. 39, 15, and 180.

Augusta laments her lover. Nos. 55, 61 (?), 72, and 129.

Released from prison, Augusta returns to her southern home to regain, after a period of grief, her old-time health and joy in life and strike out upon a new love adventure. Nos. 113, 16, 73, 74, 106, 48, 50, 51, 53, 105, and 49.

III. A.G.A. and Lord Alfred of Aspin Castle

Lord Alfred's blue-eyed, golden-haired daughter adopts a boy of sorrow. Nos. 14, 11, 186, and 187.

The girl's mother dies, and Lord Alfred marries A.G.A. Nos. 152, 153, 137, 143, and 154.

A.G.A. wins the boy to dishonorable love, and when tired of the game dismisses him in shame. No. 112.

A.G.A. deserts Lord Alfred for Julius Brenzaida. Nos. 80, 81, 162, 169, 110, and 184.

Lord Alfred, in exile, kills himself. Nos. 85 and 25.

IV. A.G.A. and Julius Brenzaida

A.G.A.'s marriage to Julius Brenzaida is the culmination of an earlier, perhaps her earliest love affair, when she was known as Rosina of Alcona. No. 178.

Julius Brenzaida, now king of Almedore, in Gaaldine, wages wars of conquest against neighboring kingdoms. Nos. 40 and 156.

Julius invades Gondal as claimant to its throne, and brings about his own coronation as joint sovereign with Gerald of the rival house of Exina. Nos. 98, 175(?), and 56.

Julius betrays Gerald. No. 125.

In the midst of Julius's triumph comes foreboding of evil. No. 12.

A conspiracy is formed to assassinate Julius, the lot of actual assassin falling to the dark-haired boy of sorrow. Nos. 179, 159, and 167(?).

The plot succeeds, but the dark boy is killed and Gleneden pays his penalty in prison. Nos. 13, 151, 63, and 97.

A.G.A. laments Julius's death. Nos. 182 and 183.

Political upheaval following Julius's assassination makes A.G.A. a fugitive with her infant daughter. Nos. 150 and 62(?).

The child dies in a mountain snowstorm. Nos. 131, 36, 108, and 100.

A.G.A. regains the throne of Gondal. No. 28.

Her triumph is clouded by loneliness and remorse. Nos. 37, 34, 82, 138, 76, and 120.

V. A.G.A. and Fernando

Augusta enslaves and betrays a youth named Fernando; the time of this episode in her life is uncertain. Nos. 33, 42, 117, 133, 134, and 123.

VI. The death of A.G.A.

Augusta is slain by Angelica and Douglas. No. 143.

Douglas outdistances his pursuers, and sends down an avalanche to engulf them. Nos. 75 and 57(?).

Lord Eldred, Captain of the Queen's Guards, laments his monarch's death. Nos. 171 and 173.

VII. Gondal poems unplaced in the story pattern

A. Poems of unidentified events. Nos. 95, 158, and 160.

B. Poems in the A.G.A. tone. Nos. 7, 79, 103, 121, 122, and 165.

C. Poems of war, imprisonment, and exile. Nos. 29, 43, 46, 58, 64, 68, 77, 83, 91, 94, 101, 102, 144, 164, 177, 189, 190, 192, and 193.

D. Poems of death and parting. Nos. 41, 52, 71, 118, 124, 130, 132, 135, 136, 139, 145, 149, 163, and 185.

E. Poems of memory and remorse. Nos. 22, 30, 38, 45, 59, 60, 86, 87, 88, 90, 142, and 172.

F. Poems of courage and defiance. Nos. 35, 146, 155, 188, and 191.

G. Poems pertaining to Gondalan institutions: The Unique Society and the Palace of Instruction. Nos. 10, 84, 104, 116, 141, and 166.

H. Poems, probably pertaining to Douglas, suggestive of Heathcliff in *Wuthering Heights*. Nos. 99, 107, and 111.

VIII. Significance of Gondal in Emily Brontë's life. Nos. 176, 140, 147, 148, 174, 27, 44, and 92.

FACSIMILE MANUSCRIPTS

Most of Emily Jane Brontë's poems manuscripts are written in very small characters (print style), and often so illegibly, and with numerous cancellations and alterations, that they are extremely difficult to read even with the aid of a magnifying glass.

Readers of this book may like to test their ability in deciphering the minute script, and to compare their readings with the printed text of the poems. As original manuscripts are rarely accessible, the following list of the books and magazines in which manuscripts of the poems of Emily Jane Brontë have been printed in facsimile may be useful. The poems so reproduced may be identified by their numbers, and the manuscript index letters and numbers within brackets, given after the name of each book or magazine.

THE WOMAN AT HOME. August, 1897. London: Hodder and Stoughton. "Relics of Emily Brontë." By Clement Shorter.
12 and 13(D2), 191(A31)

THE COMPLETE WORKS OF EMILY BRONTË. In two volumes. Vol. II: Prose. WUTHERING HEIGHTS. By Emily Brontë. With an introduction by Clement K. Shorter, and many facsimiles of Emily Brontë's handwriting. London: Hodder and Stoughton. 1911.
16 (last 5 lines), 32, 39, 40, 41, 61, 62, 86, 97 (first 3 and last 11 lines), 98, 99, 100, 102, 111, 112, 118 (C1 to 16: the whole manuscript), 141(D15)

BRONTË POEMS. Edited by Arthur C. Benson. London: Smith, Elder and Company. 1915.
182(B36), 193(B45)

A BIBLIOGRAPHY OF THE WRITINGS IN PROSE AND VERSE OF THE MEMBERS OF THE BRONTË FAMILY. By Thomas J. Wise. London: Richard Clay and Sons, Ltd. 1917.

39(C2) Lines 25–28; 40(C3) Lines 1–11; 62(C6) Lines 8–12; 100(C7) Lines 1–10; 191(A31)

THE NINETEENTH CENTURY AND AFTER. August, 1926. London: Constable and Company, Ltd. "Emily Brontë's Poems: Some Textual Corrections and Unpublished Verses." By Davidson Cook.
191(A31)

ALL ALONE: The Life and Private History of Emily Jane Brontë. By Romer Wilson. London: Chatto and Windus. 1928.
109(D3)

A BRONTË LIBRARY. Collected by Thomas J. Wise. Printed in Great Britain by the Dunedin Press, Ltd., Edinburgh. 1929.
The same pages from manuscript "C" as in the *Bibliography* of 1917

CATALOGUE OF THE BONNELL COLLECTION in the Brontë Parsonage Museum. Haworth. 1932.
15(D4) Lines 1–52

THE POEMS OF EMILY JANE BRONTË AND ANNE BRONTË. Oxford: The Shakespeare Head Press. 1934.
86, 91 to 94, 116, 120 to 123, 134 to 136, 138, 140, 146 to 149, 155, 157, 165, 168, 170, 174, 176, 181, 183, 184, 188, 191 (A1–31: the whole manuscript)

THE LIFE AND EAGER DEATH OF EMILY BRONTË. By Virginia Moore. London: Rich and Cowan, Ltd. 1936.
9(B1), 81(B14), 110(B4), 175(B33), 182(B36)

GONDAL POEMS. By Emily Jane Brontë. Edited by Helen Brown and Joan Mott. Oxford: Shakespeare Head Press. 1938.
190(B43) Lines 1–44; 192(B44) Lines 213–263

AN ORTHOGRAPHICAL NOTE

Emily Jane Brontë's spelling, in her poems manuscripts, exhibits peculiarities which it is not considered expedient to perpetuate in print. Many errors were probably due to carelessness, as in "accross," "beblow," "brouze," "buissy," etc. Some obsolete spellings, such as "gulph," "faultering," "dongeon" (usually "dongoen" in the manuscripts), have been retained.

The following are some of the words, found in the manuscripts, which have been altered to agree with ordinary spelling:—

accross	chaseing	exsist	guant
acheing	cheif	extacy	(gaunt)
adeiu	choeked		
aweful	closeing	feilds	hopeing
	comeing	feind	hopless
beblow	controul	feirce	(hopeless)
(below)	copeing	fervant	
been		firn	
(being)	dazzel	forbodeing	I'de
beleive	deifyed	forelorn	imensity
blanche	devided	foriegn	intensley
breath	devine	fortelling	
(breathe)	(divine)	freind	
broard	dieing		journy
(broad)	dimed	gardian	
brouze	(dimmed)	(guardian)	knook
(browse)	dispair	giveing	
buissy		Gommorah	laureled
(busy)	echoeing	gorey	levert
	err	greif	(leveret)
carressing	(ere)	greive	lightening
cerfew	eternaly	grive	(lightning)
(curfew)	etherial	(grieve)	lonley

majian
mared
  (marred)
matless
  (mateless)
ment
  (meant)
misterious
murmer

nurseling

oacen
  (ocean)
ore
  (o'er)
orewelmed

peirce
pineing
prehaps
  (perhaps)
purifyed

rearl
  (real)
recives
  (receives)
re-echoe
rejoiceingly
repells
repineing
rosey

sadest
  (saddest)
scatered
scearce
sceattered
shallt
sheild
shineing
skillful
skys
  (skies)
smoothe
  (smooth)

sooth
  (soothe)
souless
specteral
stareing
stoney
streching
symathy
symphathy
  (sympathy)

thrawl
tiney
toomb
tortered
  (tortured)
tyrrany
truely

vallys
vapurs
  (vapours)
virture
  (virtue)

voicless

wakeing
waneing
waveing
wavey
weaveing
were
  (where)
whach
whached
whacher
whachful
whachfuly
whaching
wholey
whreched
wistle
wonderous
wonterd
  (wonted)

yields

SOURCES FROM WHICH THE TEXT OF THE POEMS HAS BEEN DERIVED

Holograph Manuscripts

A

THE HONRESFELD MANUSCRIPT

> 29 pages containing 31 poems (A1–31)
> The first page is headed "E.J.B. Transcribed February, 1844."

There are pencilled additions in this manuscript in the hand-writing of Emily Jane Brontë and Charlotte Brontë. Those by Emily were probably made when she was selecting poems for printing in the little volume described under "G" (see below). They include the titles, "The Night-Wind," "Love and Friend-ship," "Hope," "My Comforter," "How Clear She Shines," "A Day Dream," "To Imagination," "The Philosopher's Conclusion."

B

THE BRITISH MUSEUM MANUSCRIPT (Smith Bequest)

> 68 pages containing 45 poems (B1–45)
> The first page is headed "Emily Jane Brontë. Transcribed February, 1844/GONDAL POEMS."

C

THE ASHLEY LIBRARY MANUSCRIPT

> 24 pages containing 16 poems or parts of poems (C1–16)

This manuscript is now in the British Museum. It is an incomplete manuscript, several leaves, including the first of the original book, having been removed and probably destroyed. The book appears to have been used for transcripts (fair copies) of poems from about the end of 1839. When the later transcript books ("A" and "B") were commenced, poems from it were copied into them, and when the contents of a whole leaf had been copied the leaf was removed from the book. This is the only manuscript book of poems in Emily Jane Brontë's cursive or ordinary handwriting.

D

THE BONNELL MANUSCRIPTS

67 poems or poetical studies on 16 separate leaves (D1–16)
From the library of the late Mr Henry Houston Bonnell.

Manuscripts D1–2 are now in the collection of Mrs H. H. Bonnell.

Manuscripts D3–16 were bequeathed to the Brontë Society, and are now in the Brontë Parsonage Museum at Haworth, Yorkshire.

E

THE HOWE MANUSCRIPTS

33 poems or poetical studies on 20 leaves of various shapes and sizes (E1–20)
Now in the library of the late Mr William T. H. Howe of New York and Cincinnati, recently transferred to the New York Public Library.

F

THE TEXAS UNIVERSITY MANUSCRIPTS

2 poems on 2 leaves (F1–2)
Now in the library of the University of Texas, Austin.

Other than Manuscript Sources

G

POEMS BY CURRER, ELLIS, AND ACTON BELL. London: Aylott and Jones, 8 Paternoster Row. 1846.

This book contains 21 poems by Ellis Bell (Emily Jane Brontë), with the pseudonym "ELLIS" printed at the end of each poem. Of the 21 poems, 15 were from manuscript "A," and 5 from manuscript "B" (see above).

H

WUTHERING HEIGHTS AND AGNES GREY. By Ellis and Acton Bell. A new edition revised, with a biographical notice of the authors, a selection from their literary remains, and a preface by Currer Bell. London: Smith, Elder and Company, 65 Cornhill. 1850.

This book contains 18 previously unpublished poems on pages 474–489. Charlotte Brontë obtained 8 of the poems from manuscript "A" and 9 from manuscript "B," and printed them with considerable differences in, and some additions to, the text. We print only the lines differing from, or which are not to be found in, the manuscripts. One poem, not found in any manuscript, is printed on pages 255–256 of the present volume.

J

THE COMPLETE POEMS OF EMILY BRONTË. Edited by Clement Shorter. London: Hodder and Stoughton. 1910.

Fourteen minor poems or poetical studies, first printed in this book from the holograph manuscripts, are now printed from Mr Shorter's transcripts, the location of the manuscripts being unknown to the present editor.

THE POEMS OF
EMILY JANE BRONTË

POEMS

An asterisk at the end of a line denotes a different reading of the manuscript from any which has hitherto been printed in an edition of Emily Jane Brontë's poems.[1]

A letter and figures at the head of a poem indicates the source from which the poem or poems under the heading were obtained (see list on pages 24–26).

Dıo

1.   Cold, clear, and blue, the morning heaven
Expands its arch on high;
Cold, clear, and blue, Lake Werna's water
Reflects that winter's sky.
The moon has set, but Venus shines
A silent, silvery star.

———

2.   July 12, 1836

Will the day be bright or cloudy?
Sweetly has its dawn begun;
But the heaven may shake with thunder
Ere the setting of the sun.

Lady, watch Apollo's journey:
Thus thy firstborn's course shall be—*
If his beams through summer vapours
Warm the earth all placidly,
Her days shall pass like a pleasant dream in sweet tranquillity.

If it darken, if a shadow
Quench his rays and summon rain,

[1] See note on page 35.

Flowers may open, buds may blossom:
Bud and flower alike are vain;
Her days shall pass like a mournful story in care and tears and
pain.

If the wind be fresh and free,
The wide skies clear and cloudless blue,
The woods and fields and golden flowers
Sparkling in sunshine and in dew,
Her days shall pass in Glory's light the world's drear desert
through.

———

3.   Tell me, tell me, smiling child,
What the past is like to thee?
"An Autumn evening soft and mild
With a wind that sighs mournfully."

Tell me, what is the present hour?
"A green and flowery spray
Where a young bird sits gathering its power
To mount and fly away."

And what is the future, happy one?
"A sea beneath a cloudless sun;
A mighty, glorious, dazzling sea
Stretching into infinity."

———

4.   The inspiring music's thrilling sound,
The glory of the festal day,
The glittering splendour rising round,
Have passed like all earth's joys away.

Forsaken by that Lady fair
She glides unheeding through them all
Covering her brow to hide the tear
That still, though checked, trembles to fall.

She hurries through the outer Hall
And up the stairs through galleries dim
That murmur to the breezes' call
The night-wind's lonely vesper hymn.

D10 is a manuscript of one leaf, containing Nos. 1 to 4 on one side, and
on the reverse Nos. 65 to 74.

D11

5.   December 13, 1836

High waving heather, 'neath stormy blasts bending,
Midnight and moonlight and bright shining stars;
Darkness and glory rejoicingly blending,
Earth rising to heaven and heaven descending,
Man's spirit away from its drear dongeon sending,*
Bursting the fetters and breaking the bars.

All down the mountain sides, wild forests lending
One mighty voice to the life-giving wind;
Rivers their banks in the jubilee rending,
Fast through the valleys a reckless course wending,
Wider and deeper their waters extending,*
Leaving a desolate desert behind.

Shining and lowering and swelling and dying,
Changing for ever from midnight to noon;
Roaring like thunder, like soft music sighing,
Shadows on shadows advancing and flying,
Lightning-bright flashes the deep gloom defying,
Coming as swiftly and fading as soon.

————

6.   Woods, you need not frown on me;
Spectral trees, that so dolefully
Shake your heads in the dreary sky,
You need not mock so bitterly.

J270

7.   February, 1837

Redbreast, early in the morning
Dank and cold and cloudy grey,
Wildly tender is thy music,
Chasing angry thought away.

My heart is not enraptured now,
My eyes are full of tears,
And constant sorrow on my brow
Has done the work of years.

It was not hope that wrecked at once
The spirit's calm in storm,
But a long life of solitude,
Hopes quenched and rising thoughts subdued,
A bleak November's calm.

What woke it then? A little child
Strayed from its father's cottage door,
And in the hour of moonlight wild
Laid lonely on the desert moor.

I heard it then, you heard it too,
And seraph sweet it sang to you;
But like the shriek of misery
That wild, wild music wailed to me.

J271

8.   Through the hours of yesternight
Hall and gallery blazed with light;
Every lamp its lustre showered
On the adorer and the adored.
None were sad that entered there,

All were loved, and all were fair;
Some were dazzling, like the sun
Shining down at summer noon;
Some were sweet as amber even,
Living in the depth of heaven;
Some were soft, and kind, and gay,
Morning's face not more divine;
Some were like Diana's day,
Midnight moonlight's holy shrine.

B1

9.   A.G.A.[1]   March 6, 1837

There shines the moon, at noon of night—
Vision of glory—Dream of light!
Holy as heaven—undimmed and pure,
Looking down on the lonely moor—
And lonelier still beneath her ray
That drear moor stretches far away
Till it seems strange that aught can lie
Beyond its zone of silver sky.

Bright moon—dear moon! when years have past
10 My weary feet return at last—
And still upon Lake Elnor's breast *
Thy solemn rays serenely rest
And still the fern-leaves sighing wave
Like mourners over Elbë's grave
And Earth's the same but oh to see
How wildly Time has altered me!
Am I the being who long ago
Sat watching by that water side,
The light of life expiring slow
20 From his fair cheek and brow of pride?
Not oft these mountains feel the shine

[1] Augusta G. Almeda.

Of such a day—as, fading then,
Cast from its fount of gold divine
A last smile on the heathery plain,
And kissed the far-off peaks of snow
That gleaming on the horizon shone
As if in summer's warmest glow
Stern winter claimed a loftier throne—
And there he lay among the bloom
30 His red blood dyed a deeper hue,
Shuddering to feel the ghostly gloom
That coming Death around him threw—
Sickening to think one hour would sever
The sweet, sweet world and him for ever,
To think that twilight gathering dim
Would never pass away to him—
No—never more! That awful thought
A thousand dreary feelings brought,
And memory all her powers combined
40 And rushed upon his fainting mind.
Wide, swelling woodlands seemed to rise
Beneath soft, sunny southern skies—
Old Elbë Hall, his noble home,
Towered 'mid its trees, whose foliage green
Rustled with the kind airs that come
From summer heavens when most serene,
And bursting through the leafy shade
A gush of golden sunshine played,
Bathing the walls in amber light
50 And sparkling in the water clear
That stretched below—reflected bright
The whole wide world of cloudless air—
And still before his spirit's eye
Such well-known scenes would rise and fly
Till, maddening with despair and pain
He turned his dying face to me
And wildly cried, "Oh, once again
Might I my native country see!

But once again—one single day!—
60 And must it—can it *never* be?
To die—and die so far away
When life has hardly smiled for me.
Augusta—you will soon return
Back to that land in health and bloom
And then the heath alone will mourn
Above my unremembered tomb,
For you'll forget the lonely grave
And mouldering corpse by Elnor's wave." *

*   *   *   *   *   *   *   *   *   *

No. 9 has not previously been printed in an edition of the poems, but
it has been printed in a book of 47 pages, *Gondal Poems* (Shakespeare
Head Press, 1938), which contained the unpublished parts of manuscript "B."

J282

10.   All day I've toiled, but not with pain,
In learning's golden mine;
And now at eventide again
The moonbeams softly shine.

There is no snow upon the ground,
No frost on wind or wave;
The south wind blew with gentlest sound
And broke their icy grave.

'Tis sweet to wander here at night
To watch the winter die,
With heart as summer sunshine light
And warm as summer sky.

O may I never lose the peace
That lulls me gently now,
Though time should change my youthful face,
And years should shade my brow!

True to myself, and true to all,
May I be healthful still,
And turn away from passion's call,
And curb my own wild will.

J252

II.   May 17, 1837

I am the only being whose doom
No tongue would ask, no eye would mourn;
I never caused a thought of gloom,
A smile of joy, since I was born.

In secret pleasure, secret tears,
This changeful life has slipped away,
As friendless after eighteen years,
As lone as on my natal day.

There have been times I cannot hide,
There have been times when this was drear,
When my sad soul forgot its pride
And longed for one to love me here.

But those were in the early glow
Of feelings since subdued by care; *
And they have died so long ago,
I hardly now believe they were.

First melted off the hope of youth,
Then fancy's rainbow fast withdrew;
And then experience told me truth
In mortal bosoms never grew.

'Twas grief enough to think mankind
All hollow, servile, insincere;
But worse to trust to my own mind
And find the same corruption there.

D2

The night of storms has passed,
The sunshine bright and clear
Gives glory to the verdant waste
And warms the breezy air;

And I would leave my bed,
Its cheering smile to see,
To chase the visions from my head
Whose forms have troubled me.

In all the hours of gloom
My soul was wrapt away; *
I dreamt I stood by a marble tomb
Where royal corpses lay.

It was just the time of eve
When parted ghosts might come
Above their prisoned dust to grieve
And wail their woeful doom.

And truly at my side
I saw a shadowy thing
Most dim, and yet its presence there
Curdled my blood with ghastly fear
And ghastlier wondering.

My breath I could not draw,
The air seemed ranny; [1] *
But still my eyes with maddening gaze
Were fixed upon its fearful face,
And its were fixed on me.

[1] A north of England colloquialism, meaning "sharp" or "keen."

I fell down on the stone,
But could [not] turn away;
My words died in a voiceless moan
When I began to pray.

And still it bent above,
Its features full in view;
It seemed close by, and yet more far
Than this world from the farthest star
That tracks the boundless blue.

Indeed, 'twas not the space
Of earth or time between,
But the sea of death's eternity,*
The gulph o'er which mortality
Has never, never been.

O bring not back again
The horror of that hour
When its lips opened, and a sound
Awoke the stillness reigning round,
Faint as a dream, but the earth shrank
And heaven's lights shivered 'neath its power.

13.   "Woe for the day; Regina's pride,
Regina's hope is in the grave;
And who shall rule my land beside,
And who shall save?

"Woe for the day; with gory tears
My country's sons this day shall rue.
Woe for the day; a thousand years
Can not repair what one shall do.

"Woe for the day." Mixt with the wind,*
That sad lament was ringing;
It almost broke my heart to hear
Such dreary, dreary singing.

*   *   *   *   *   *   *   *   *

I saw thee, child, one summer's day *
Suddenly leave thy cheerful play,
And in the green grass, lowly lying,
I listened to thy mournful sighing.

I knew the wish that waked that wail;
I knew the source whence sprung those tears;
You longed for fate to raise the veil
That darkened over coming years.

The anxious prayer was heard, and power
10 Was given me, in that silent hour,
To open to an infant's eye
The portals of futurity.

But, child of dust, the fragrant flowers,
The bright blue sky and velvet sod
Were strange conductors to the bowers
Thy daring footsteps must have trod.

I watched my time, and summer passed,
And Autumn waning fleeted by,
And doleful winter nights at last
20 In cloudy mourning clothed the sky.*

And now I'm come: this evening fell
Not stormily, but stilly drear;
A sound sweeps o'er thee like a knell
To banish joy and welcome care;

A fluttering blast that shakes the leaves,
And whistles round the gloomy wall,
And lingering long lamenting grieves,*
For 'tis the spectre's call.

He hears me: what a sudden start
30 Sent the blood icy to that heart; *
He wakens, and how ghastly white
That face looks in the dim lamplight.

Those tiny hands in vain essay
To thrust the shadowy fiend away;
There is a horror on his brow,
An anguish in his bosom now;

A fearful anguish in his eyes
Fixed strainedly on the vacant air;
Heavily bursts in long-drawn sighs *
40 His panting breath, enchained by fear.

Poor child, if spirits such as I
Could weep o'er human misery,
A tear might flow, aye, many a tear,
To see the road that lies before,
To see the sunshine disappear,
And hear the stormy waters roar,
Breaking upon a desolate shore,
Cut off from hope in early day,
From power and glory cut away.

50 But it is doomed, and morning's light
Must image forth the scowl of night,
And childhood's flower must waste its bloom
Beneath the shadow of the tomb.

D4

15.   August 7, 1837
                                                  E.J.B.[1]

O God of heaven! the dream of horror,
The frightful dream is over now;

[1] The author's initials.

The sickened heart, the blasting sorrow,
The ghastly night, the ghastlier morrow,
The aching sense of utter woe;

The burning tears that would keep welling,
The groans that mocked at every tear *
That burst from out their dreary dwelling
As if each gasp were life expelling,
10 But life was nourished by despair;

The tossing and the anguished pining;
The grinding teeth and staring eye; *
The agony of still repining,
When not a spark of hope was shining
From gloomy fate's relentless sky;

The impatient rage, the useless shrinking
From thoughts that yet could not be borne;
The soul that was for ever thinking,
Till nature, maddened, tortured, sinking,
20 At last refused to mourn—

It's over now—and I am free,
And the ocean wind is caressing me,
The wild wind from that wavy main
I never thought to see again.

Bless thee, Bright Sea—and glorious dome,
And my own world, my spirit's home;
Bless thee, Bless all—I can not speak:
My voice is choked, but not with grief;
And salt drops from my haggard cheek
30 Descend, like rain upon the heath.

How long they've wet a dongeon floor,*
Falling on flag-stones damp and grey!
I used to weep even in my sleep;
The night was dreadful, like the day.

I used to weep when winter's snow
Whirled through the grating stormily,
But then it was a calmer woe
For everything was drear as me.*

The bitterest time, the worst of all,
40 Was that in which the summer sheen
Cast a green luster on the wall
That told of fields of lovelier green.

Often I've sat down on the ground,
Gazing up to that flush scarce seen,
Till, heedless of the darkness round,
My soul has sought a land serene.

It sought the arch of heaven divine,
The pure blue heaven with clouds of gold;
It sought thy father's home and mine
50 As I remembered it of old.

O even now too horribly
Come back the feelings that would swell,
When with my face hid on my knee
I strove the bursting groans to quell.

I flung myself upon the stone,
I howled and tore my tangled hair,
And then, when the first gush had flown,*
Lay in unspeakable despair.

Sometimes a curse, sometimes a prayer
60 Would quiver on my parchèd tongue;
But both without a murmur there
Died in the breast from whence they sprung.

And so the day would fade on high,
And darkness quench that lonely beam,

And slumber mould my misery
Into some strange and spectral dream
Whose phantom horrors made me know
The worst extent of human woe—

But this is past, and why return
70 O'er such a past to brood and mourn? *
Shake off the fetters, break the chain,
And live and love and smile again.

The waste of youth, the waste of years,
Departed in that dongeon's thrall; *
The gnawing grief, the hopeless tears,
Forget them—O forget them all.

B2

16.   A.G.A. TO A.E.[1]   E.[2]   August 19, 1837

Lord of Elbë, on Elbë hill
The mist is thick and the wind is chill
And the heart of thy Friend from the dawn of day *
Has sighed for sorrow that thou went away.*

Lord of Elbë, how pleasant to me
The sound of thy blithesome step would be
Rustling the heath that, only now
Waves as the night-gusts over it blow.*

Bright are the fires in thy lonely home *
I see them far off, and as deepens the gloom
Gleaming like stars through the high forest-boughs *
Gladder they glow in the park's repose.

[1] Alexander Elbë.
[2] Probably the author's initial.

O Alexander! when I return,
Warm as those hearths my heart would burn,*
Light as thine own, my foot would fall *
If I might hear thy voice in the hall.

But thou art now on a desolate sea—
Parted from Gondal and parted from me—*
All my repining is hopeless and vain,*
Death never yields back his victims again.*

D6

SONG   August 19, 1837   A.G.A.

Lord of Elbe, on Elbe hill
Line 3 And the heart of thy friend from the dawning of day
      8 Moans as the night gusts over it blow
      9 Bright are the fires in thy noble home
     11 Shining like stars through the high forest boughs
     15 Light as thine own my step would fall
     17 But thou art now on the desolate sea
     18 Thinking of Gondal and grieving for me
     19 Longing to be in sweet Elbe again
     20 Thinking and grieving and longing in vain

The whole poem in this manuscript is heavily cancelled by lines drawn
across it.

C1

[*Lord of Elbë, on Elbë hill*]

The last 5 lines only are in this manuscript:

If I might hear thy voice in the hall

But thou art now on a desolate sea
Thinking of Gondal, and grieving for me;
Longing to be in sweet Elbë again,
Thinking and grieving and longing in vain.

E. J. Brontë—August 19, 1837

This manuscript gives the following interlined reading of the last
3 lines:

> Parted from Gondal, and parted from me;
> All my repining is hopeless and vain;
> Death never gives back his victim again.*

D12

17.   August, 1837

> The battle had passed from the height,
> And still did evening fall;
> While heaven, with its hosts of night,*
> Gloriously canopied all.
>
> The dead around were sleeping
> On heath and granite grey;
> And the dying their last watch were keeping
> In the closing of the day.

*   *   *   *   *   *

18.   How golden bright from earth and heaven
> The summer day declines;
> How gloriously o'er land and sea
> The parting sunbeam shines.
>
> There is a voice in the wind that waves
> Those bright rejoicing trees.

*   *   *

19.   Not a vapour had stained the breezeless blue,
> Not a cloud had dimmed the sun
> From the time of morning's earliest dew
> Till the summer day was done;
>
> And all as pure and all as bright
> The beam of evening died; *

And purer still its parting light
Shone in Lake Elnor's tide.*

Waveless and calm lies that silent deep
In its wilderness of moors;
Solemn and soft the moonbeams sleep
Upon its heathy shores.

The deer are gathered to their rest,
The wild sheep seek the fold.

*   *   *

20.   Only some spires of bright green grass
        Transparently in sunshine quivering

———

21.   The sun has set, and the long grass now
        Waves drearily in the evening wind; *
        And the wild bird has flown from that old grey stone,
        In some warm nook a couch to find.

        In all the lonely landscape round
        I see no sight and hear no sound,*
        Except the wind that far away
        Comes sighing o'er the heathy sea.

———

22.   Lady, in your Palace Hall,
        Once, perchance, my face was seen; *
        Can no memory now recall
        Thought again to what has been?

———

23.   And first an hour of mournful musing,
        And then a gush of bitter tears,
        And then a dreary calm diffusing
        Its deadly mist o'er joys and cares;

Except for you the billowy sea
Would now be tossing under me
The winds wild voice my bosom thrill
And my glad heart bound wilder still.

Flying before the rapid gale
These windows southern isles to hail
Which wait for my companions free
But mock your passion - not for me!

You know too well - and so do I
Your haughty beauty's sovereignty
Yet love I with these falcon eyes -
Have dived into their mystic mysteries -
Have studied long their glance and feel
It is not love those eyes reveal -

They flash, they burn with lightning shine
But not with such fond love as mine,

The tender star fades faint and wan
Before Ambition's scorching sun -
So deem I now - and Time will prove
If I have wronged Rosina's love -

Dec 2d 1844 - ⚓ From a D.W. in the N C.   A G A. Sept - 1826.

"O Day, He cannot die
"When thou art so fair and shining.
"O sun, in such a glorious sky
"So gloriously declining,

"He cannot leave thee now
"While fresh west winds are blowing
"And all around his youthful brow
"Thy crystal light is glowing!

"Edith, awake, awake!
"The golden evening gleams
"and bright on Elbë's lake,
"Arouse thee from thy dreams!

"down, on my knee,
"My own dearfriend, I pray
"That thou wilt cross the stormy sea
"Wildly it cold thou delay!

"I hear its billows roar
"I see them foaming high
"But no glimpse of a further shore
"Has blessed my straining eye -

And then a throb, and then a lightening,
And then a breathing from above,*
And then a star in heaven brightening—
The star, the glorious star of love.

———

24.   Wind, sink to rest in the heather,
Thy wild voice suits not me:
I would have dreary weather,
But all devoid of thee.

Sun, set from that evening heaven,
Thy glad smile wins not mine;
If light at all is given,
O give me Cynthia's shine.

———

25.   Long neglect has worn away
Half the sweet enchanting smile; *
Time has turned the bloom to grey;
Mould and damp the face defile.

But that lock of silky hair,
Still beneath the picture twined,
Tells what once those features were,
Paints their image on the mind.

Fair the hand that traced that line,
"Dearest, ever deem me true";
Swiftly flew the fingers fine
When the pen that motto drew.

———

26.   Awaking morning laughs from heaven
On golden summer's forests green;
And what a gush of song is given *
To welcome in that light serene.

A fresh wind waves the clustering roses,
And through the open window sighs
Around the couch where she reposes,
The lady with the dovelike eyes;

With dovelike eyes and shining hair,
And velvet cheek so sweetly moulded;
And hands so soft and white and fair
Above her snowy bosom folded.

* * *

Her sister's and her brother's feet
Are brushing off the scented dew,
And she springs up in haste to greet
The grass and flowers and sunshine too.

———

The asterisks and lines under D12 are given as they appear in the
manuscript. On one side of the manuscript leaf are Nos. 17 to 22, and on
the reverse Nos. 23 to 26.

D6

27.   August, 1837

Alone I sat; the summer day
Had died in smiling light away;
I saw it die, I watched it fade
From misty hill and breezeless glade;

And thoughts in my soul were gushing,*
And my heart bowed beneath their power;
And tears within my eyes were rushing *
Because I could not speak the feeling,
The solemn joy around me stealing
In that divine, untroubled hour.

I asked myself, "O why has heaven
Denied the precious gift to me,

The glorious gift to many given
To speak their thoughts in poetry?

"Dreams have encircled me," I said,
"From careless childhood's sunny time;
Visions by ardent fancy fed
Since life was in its morning prime."

But now, when I had hoped to sing,
My fingers strike a tuneless string;
And still the burden of the strain
Is "Strive no more; 'tis all in vain."

Manuscript D6 is a single leaf containing Nos. 27, 36, 37, and 38 on one side, and cancelled versions of Nos. 40, 62, and 16 respectively on the reverse.

F1

28.   September 30, 1837

The organ swells, the trumpets sound,
The lamps in triumph glow;
And none of all those thousands round
Regards who sleeps below.*

Those haughty eyes that tears should fill
Glance clearly, cloudlessly;
Those bounding breasts, that grief should thrill,
From thought of grief are free.

His subjects and his soldiers there
They blessed his rising bloom,
But none a single sigh can spare
To breathe above his tomb.

Comrades in arms, I've looked to mark
One shade of feeling swell,

As your feet trod above the dark *
Recesses of his cell.

J254

29.   October 14, 1837

A sudden chasm of ghastly light
Yawned in the city's reeling wall,
And a long thundering through the night
Proclaimed our triumph—Tyndarum's fall.

The shrieking wind sank mute and mild;
The smothering snow-clouds rolled away;
And cold—how cold!—wan moonlight smiled
Where those black ruins smouldering lay.

'Twas over—all the battle's madness,
10   The bursting fires, the cannons' roar,
The yells, the groans, the frenzied gladness,
The death, the danger, alarmed no more.

In plundered churches piled with dead
The heavy charger neighed for food;
The wounded soldier laid his head
'Neath roofless chambers splashed with blood.

I could not sleep: through that wild siege
My heart had fiercely burned and bounded;
The outward tumult seemed to assuage
20   The inward tempest it surrounded.
                    .   .   .   .

But dreams like this I cannot bear,
And silence whets the fang of pain;
I felt the full flood of despair
Returning to my breast again.

My couch lay in a ruined Hall,
Whose windows looked on the minster-yard,
Where chill, chill whiteness covered all—
Both stone and urn and withered sward.

The shattered glass let in the air,
30 And with it came a wandering moan,
A sound unutterably drear
That made me shrink to be alone.

One black yew-tree grew just below—
I thought its boughs so sad might wail;
Their ghostly fingers, flecked with snow,
Rattled against an old vault's rail.

I listened—no; 'twas life that still
Lingered in some deserted heart:
O God! what caused the shuddering shrill,
40 That anguished, agonising start?

An undefined, an awful dream,
A dream of what had been before;
A memory whose blighting beam
Was flitting o'er me evermore.

A frightful feeling, frenzy born—
I hurried down the dark oak stair;
I reached the door whose hinges torn
Flung streaks of moonshine here and there.

I pondered not; I drew the bar;
50 An icy glory caught mine eye,
From that wide heaven where every star
Stared like a dying memory;

And there the great Cathedral rose
Discrowned but most majestic so,
It looked down in serene repose
On its own realm of buried woe.

E2

30. 'Tis evening now, the sun descends
In golden glory down the sky;
The city's murmur softly blends
With zephyrs breathing gently by.

And yet it seems a dreary morn,*
A dark October morn to me,*
And black the piles of rain-clouds born *
Athwart heaven's stormy canopy.

The above two verses are on a separate scrap of paper. They have hitherto been printed as the last two verses of No. 29.

J274

31.   October, 1837

The old church tower and garden wall
Are black with autumn rain,
And dreary winds foreboding call
The darkness down again.

I watched how evening took the place
Of glad and glorious day;
I watched a deeper gloom efface
The evening's lingering ray.

And as I gazed on the cheerless sky
Sad thoughts rose in my mind. . . .

C15

32. <div style="text-align:center">LINES</div> October, 1837

Far away is the land of rest,
Thousand miles are stretched between,
Many a mountain's stormy crest,
Many a desert void of green.

Wasted, worn is the traveller;
Dark his heart and dim his eye;
Without hope or comforter,
Faultering, faint, and ready to die.

Often he looks to the ruthless sky,
Often he looks o'er his dreary road,
Often he wishes down to lie
And render up life's tiresome load.

But yet faint not, mournful man;
Leagues on leagues are left behind
Since your sunless course began;
Then go on to toil resigned.

If you still despair control,
Hush its whispers in your breast,
You shall reach the final goal,
You shall win the land of rest.

D11

33. November, 1837

Now trust a heart that trusts in you,
And firmly say the word "Adieu";
Be sure, wherever I may roam,
My heart is with your heart at home;

Unless there be no truth on earth,
And vows meant true are nothing worth,*
And mortal man have no control
Over his own unhappy soul;

Unless I change in every thought,
And memory will restore me nought,
And all I have of virtue die
Beneath far Gondal's Foreign sky.

The mountain peasant loves the heath
Better than richest plains beneath;
He would not give one moorland wild
For all the fields that ever smiled;

And whiter brows than yours may be,
And rosier cheeks my eyes may see,
And lightning looks from orbs divine
About my pathway burn and shine;

But that pure light, changeless and strong,
Cherished and watched and nursed so long;
That love that first its glory gave
Shall be my pole star to the grave.

———

34.   November, 1837   A.G.A.

Sleep brings no joy to me,
Remembrance never dies;
My soul is given to misery
And lives in sighs.

Sleep brings no rest to me;
The shadows of the dead
My waking eyes may never see *
Surround my bed.

Sleep brings no hope to me;
In soundest sleep they come,
And with their doleful imagery
Deepen the gloom.

Sleep brings no strength to me,
No power renewed to brave,
I only sail a wilder sea,
A darker wave.

Sleep brings no friend to me
To soothe and aid to bear;
They all gaze, oh, how scornfully,*
And I despair.

Sleep brings no wish to knit *
My harassed heart beneath;
My only wish is to forget
In sleep of death.*

The last line in the manuscript reads, "In the sleep of death."

---

35.   Strong I stand, though I have borne
Anger, hate, and bitter scorn;
Strong I stand, and laugh to see
How mankind have fought with me.

Shade of mast'ry, I contemn *
All the puny ways of men;
Free my heart, my spirit free;
Beckon, and I'll follow thee.

False and foolish mortal, know,
If you scorn the world's disdain,
Your mean soul is far below
Other worms, however vain.

Thing of Dust—with boundless pride,
Dare you take me for a guide? *
With the humble I will be;
Haughty men are nought to me.

Manuscript D11 is one leaf containing Nos. 33, 34, and 35 on one side, and on the reverse Nos. 82, 83, 84, 5, and 6 respectively.

D6

36.   November, 1837

The night is darkening round me,
The wild winds coldly blow;
But a tyrant spell has bound me
And I cannot, cannot go.

The giant trees are bending
Their bare boughs weighed with snow,
And the storm is fast descending
And yet I cannot go.

Clouds beyond clouds above me,
Wastes beyond wastes below;
But nothing drear can move me;
I will not, cannot go.

37.   I'll come when thou art saddest,
Laid alone in the darkened room; *
When the mad day's mirth has vanished,*
And the smile of joy is banished
From evening's chilly gloom.

I'll come when the heart's real feeling *
Has entire, unbiassed sway,
And my influence o'er thee stealing,
Grief deepening, joy congealing,
Shall bear thy soul away.

Listen, 'tis just the hour,
The awful time for thee;
Dost thou not feel upon thy soul
A flood of strange sensations roll,
Forerunners of a sterner power,
Heralds of me?

———

38.   I would have touched the heavenly key
That spoke alike of bliss and thee;
I would have woke the entrancing song,*
But its words died upon my tongue;
And then I knew that entheal [1] strain *
Could never speak of joy again; *
And then I felt . . . . [unfinished]

C2

39.   TO A WREATH OF SNOW

By A. G. Almeda

O transient voyager of heaven!
O silent sign of winter skies!
What adverse wind thy sail has driven
To dungeons where a prisoner lies?

Methinks the hands that shut the sun
So sternly from this mourning brow
Might still their rebel task have done
And checked a thing so frail as thou.

They would have done it had they known
The talisman that dwelt in thee,
For all the suns that ever shone
Have never been so kind to me.

[1] Or "hallowed."

For many a week, and many a day,
My heart was weighed with sinking gloom,
When morning rose in mourning grey
And faintly lit my prison room;

But, angel like, when I awoke,
Thy silvery form so soft and fair,
Shining through darkness, sweetly spoke
Of cloudy skies and mountains bare—

The dearest to a mountaineer,
Who, all life long has loved the snow
That crowned her native summits drear *
Better than greenest plains below.

And, voiceless, soulless messenger,
Thy presence waked a thrilling tone
That comforts me while thou art here
And will sustain when thou art gone.

Emily Jane Brontë, December —, 1837

E13

[O transient voyager of heaven]

A manuscript, the lower half of a torn leaf, containing on one side
the last seven lines of No. 39, cancelled by lines drawn across them.
Below the lines is No. 44, and on the reverse of the half leaf is No. 43.

C3

40.   SONG BY JULIUS ANGORA

Awake! awake! how loud the stormy morning
Calls up to life the nations resting round;
Arise! arise! is it the voice of mourning
That breaks our slumber with so wild a sound?

The voice of mourning? Listen to its pealing;
That shout of triumph drowns the sigh of woe.
Each tortured heart forgets its wonted feeling;
Each faded cheek resumes its long-lost glow.

Our souls are full of gladness; God has given
Our arms to victory, our foes to death;
The crimson ensign waves its sheet in heaven,
The sea-green Standard lies in dust beneath.

Patriots, no stain is on your country's glory;
Soldiers, preserve that glory bright and free.
Let Almedore, in peace, and battle gory,
Be still a nobler name for victory!

D6

Another manuscript of No. 40.

SONG   December, 1837
                                        J.A.[1]

Awake awake how loud the stormy morning

The text agrees with that printed above. The lines are cancelled in
this manuscript.

C8

41.   LINES   December, 1837

I die; but when the grave shall press
The heart so long endeared to thee,
When earthly cares no more distress
And earthly joys are nought to me,

Weep not, but think that I have past
Before thee o'er a sea of gloom,

[1] Julius Angora.

Have anchored safe, and rest at last
Where tears and mourning cannot come.

'Tis I should weep to leave thee here,
On that dark Ocean, sailing drear,
With storms around and fears before
And no kind light to point the shore.

But long or short though life may be
'Tis nothing to eternity;
We part below to meet on high
Where blissful ages never die.

D9

42.   December 14, 1837

O mother, I am not regretting
To leave this wretched world below,
If there be nothing but forgetting
In that dark land to which I go.

Yet though 'tis wretched now to languish,
Deceived and tired and hopeless here,
No heart can quite repress the anguish
Of leaving things that once were dear.

Twice twelve short years, and all is over,
10 And day and night to rise no more;
And never more to be a rover
Along the fields, the woods, the shore;

And never more at early dawning
To watch the stars of midnight wane;
To breathe the breath of summer morning
And see its sunshine ne'er again.

I hear the Abbey bells are ringing:
Methinks their chime-sound faint and drear,*
Or else the wind is adverse winging,
20 And wafts its music from my ear.

The wind the winter night is speaking
Of thoughts and things that should not stay;
Mother, come near; my heart is breaking;
I cannot bear to go away.

And I *must* go whence no returning *
To soothe your grief or calm your care;
Nay, do not weep: that bitter mourning
Tortures my soul with wild despair.

No; tell me that, when I am lying
30 In the old church beneath the stone,
You'll dry your tears and check your sighing,
And soon forget the spirit gone.

You've asked me long to tell what sorrow
Has blanched my cheek and quenched my eye;
And we shall sever ere to-morrow,*
So I'll confess before I die.

Ten years ago in last September
Fernando left his home and you,
And still I think you must remember
40 The anguish of that last adieu;

And well you know how, wildly pining,
I longed to see his face again
Through all the Autumn's drear declining,*
Its stormy nights and days of rain.

Down on the skirts of Areon's forest
There lies a lone and lovely glade;

And there the hearts together nourished
Their first, their fatal parting made.

The afternoon, in softened glory,
50 Bathed each green swell and waving tree;
Beyond the broad park, spread before me,*
Stretched far away the boundless sea.*

And there I stood, when he had left me,
With ashy cheek but tearless eye,*
Watching the ship whose sail bereft me
Of life and hope and peace and joy.*

It past; that night I sought a pillow
Of sleepless woe, and grieving lone
My soul still hovered o'er the billow,*
60 And mourned a love for ever flown.

Yet, smiling bright in recollection,
One blissful hour returns to me:
One letter told of firm affection,*
Of safe deliverance from the sea;

But not another. Fearing, hoping,
Spring, winter, harvest, glided o'er;
And time at length brought power for coping
With thoughts I could not once endure.

And I would seek in summer's evening
70 The place that saw our last farewell;
And there, a chain of visions weaving,
I'd linger till the curfew bell.

* * * * * *

Manuscript D9 is a single leaf, with the first 12 verses of No. 42 on one
side, and on the reverse the remaining 6 verses, followed by the 5 verses
of No. 60.

E13

43. February H.G. 1838

Weaned from life and torn away *
In the morning of thy day;
Bound in everlasting gloom;
Buried in a hopeless tomb; *

Yet upon thy bended knee
Thank the power [that] banished thee;
Chain and bar and dongeon wall *
Saved thee from a deadlier thrall.

Thank the power that made thee part
Ere that parting broke thy heart.

Wildly rushed the mountain spring
From its source of fern and ling;
How invincible its roar
Had its waters won the shore.*

* * * * * * * * *

The last four lines have been printed as a separate fragment, but there
is no dividing line in the manuscript.

44. I'm happiest when most away *
I can bear my soul from its home of clay *
On a windy night when the moon is bright
And the eye can wander through worlds of light—*

When I am not and none beside—
Nor earth nor sea nor cloudless sky—
But only spirit wandering wide
Through infinite immensity.

E8

45. All hushed and still within the house;
    Without—all wind and driving rain;
    But something whispers to my mind,
    Through rain and through the wailing wind,*
        Never again.*
    Never again? Why not again? *
    Memory has power as real as thine.*

———

46. Iernë's eyes were glazed and dim
    When the castle bell tolled one.
    She looked around her dungeon grim;
    The grating cast a doubtful gleam;
    'Twas one cloud-saddened cold moon-beam.
    Iernë gazed as in a dream
    And thought she saw the sun.

    She thought it was the break of day,
    The night had been so long.

  No. 46 is cancelled by lines drawn across it in the manuscript.

F2

47. But the hearts that once adored me
    Have long forgot their vow;
    And the friends that mustered round me
    Have all forsaken now.

    'Twas in a dream revealed to me,
    But not a dream of sleep:
    A dream of watchful agony,
    Of grief that would not weep.*

Now do not harshly turn away,
B . . . [unfinished]

Manuscripts E8 and F2 were originally a single leaf, E8 being the upper half of the leaf. Hitherto No. 47 has been printed as a continuation of No. 45.

D5

48. Deep, deep down in the silent grave,
With none to mourn above.

———

49. Here, with my knee upon thy stone,
I bid adieu to feelings gone;
I leave with thee my tears and pain,
And rush into the world again.

———

50. O come again; what chains withhold
The steps that used so fleet to be?
Come, leave thy dwelling dank and cold *
Once more to visit me.

———

51. Was it with the fields of green,
Blowing flower and budding tree,
With the summer heaven serene,
That thou didst visit me?

No; 'twas not the flowery plain;
No; 'twas not the fragrant air:
Summer skies will come again,
But *thou* wilt not be there.*

———

52. How loud the storm sounds round the Hall!
From arch to arch, from door to door,

Pillar and roof and granite wall
Rock like a cradle in its roar.

That elm tree by the haunted well
Greets no returning summer skies:
Down with a rush the giant fell,
And stretched athwart the path it lies.

Hardly had passed the funeral train,
So long delayed by wind and snow;
And how they'll reach the house again
To-morrow's dawn perhaps will show.*

———

53.   What use is it to slumber here,
Though the heart be sad and weary?
What use is it to slumber here,
Though the day rise dark and dreary?

For that mist may break when the sun is high,
And this soul forget its sorrow;
And the rosy ray of the closing day
May promise a brighter morrow.

———

54.   O evening, why is thy light so sad?
Why is the sun's last ray so cold?
Hush; our smile is as ever glad,
But thy heart is growing old.

Manuscript D5 is a single leaf, with Nos. 48 to 54 on one side, and on
the reverse Nos. 55 to 57.

55.   It's over now; I've known it all;
I'll hide it in my heart no more,
But back again that night recall,
And think the fearful vision o'er.

The evening sun, in cloudless shine,
Had pass'd from summer's heaven divine;
And dark the shades of twilight grew,
And stars were in the depth of blue;

And in the heath on mountains far
From human eye and human care,
With thoughtful heart and tearful eye
I sadly watched that solemn sky.

———

56.   March, 1838

The wide cathedral aisles [1] are lone,
The vast crowds vanished, every one;
There can be nought beneath that dome
But the cold tenants of the tomb.

O look again, for still on high
The lamps are burning gloriously;
And look again, for still beneath
A thousand thousand live and breathe.

All mute as death regard the shrine *
That gleams in lustre so divine,
Where Gondal's monarchs, bending low
After the hush of silent prayer,*
Take, in heaven's sight, their awful vow,
And never dying union swear.
King Julius lifts his impious eye
From the dark marble to the sky;
Blasts with that Oath his perjured soul,
And changeless is his cheek the while,
Though burning thoughts, that spurn control,
Kindle a short and bitter smile,

[1] "Isles" in the manuscript (Obs.).

As face to face the kinsmen stand,*
His false hand clasped in Gerald's hand.

* * * * * * * * *

57.   O hinder me by no delay,
My horse is weary of the way;
And still his breast must stem the tide
Whose waves are foaming far and wide.
Leagues off I heard their thundering roar,
As fast they burst upon the shore:
A stronger steed than mine might dread
To brave them in their boiling bed.

Thus spoke the traveller, but in vain:
The stranger would not turn away;
Still clung she to his bridle rein,
And still entreated him to stay.

* * * *

J272

58.   May, 1838

Darkness was overtraced on every face;
Around clouded with storm and ominous gloom;
In hut or hall there was no resting-place;
There was no resting-place but one—the tomb!

All our hearts were the mansions of distress,
And no one laughed, and none seemed free from care;
Our children felt their fathers' wretchedness;
Our homes, one, all were shadowed with despair.

It was not fear that made the land so sad. . . .
                                        [unfinished]

J273

59. Harp of wild and dream-like strain,
When I touch thy strings,
Why dost thou repeat again
Long-forgotten things?

Harp, in other, earlier days,
I could sing to thee;
And not one of all my lays
Vexed my memory.

But now, if I awake a note
That gave me joy before,
Sounds of sorrow from thee float,
Changing evermore.

Yet, still steeped in memory's dyes,
They come sailing on,
Darkening all my summer skies,
Shutting out my sun.

D9

60.   A.G.A.   May 9, 1838

Why do I hate that lone green dell?
Buried in moors and mountains wild,
That is a spot I had loved too well
Had I but seen it when a child.

There are bones whitening there in the summer's heat,*
But it is not for that, and none can tell;
None but one can the secret repeat
Why I hate that lone green dell.

Noble foe, I pardon thee
All thy cold and scornful pride,
For thou wast a priceless friend to me
When my sad heart had none beside.

And, leaning on thy generous arm,
A breath of old times over me came;
The earth shone round with a long-lost charm;
Alas, I forgot I was not the same.

Before a day—an hour—passed by,
My spirit knew itself once more;
I saw the gilded vapours fly *
And leave me as I was before.

B6

61.   A.G.A. to A.S.   E.   May 20, 1838

O wander not so far away!
O love, forgive this selfish tear—
It may be sad for thee to stay,
But how can I live lonely here?

The still May morn is warm and bright,
Young flowers look fresh and grass is green; *
And in the haze of glorious light
Our long, low hills are scarcely seen.

The woods—even now their small leaves hide *
The blackbird and the stockdove well; *
And high in heaven, so blue and wide,
A thousand strains of music swell.

He looks on all with eyes that speak
So deep, so drear a woe to me!
There is a faint red on his cheek
Not like the bloom I used to see.

Call [1] Death—yes, Death, he is thine own!
The grave must close those limbs around,
And hush, for ever hush the tone
I loved above all earthly sound.

Well, pass away with the other flowers:
Too dark for them, too dark for thee
Are the hours to come, the joyless hours,
That Time is treasuring up for me.

If thou hast sinned in this world of care,
'Twas but the dust of thy drear abode—
Thy soul was pure when it entered here,
And pure it will go again to God.

No. 61 is dated February 20, 1838, in previous editions, as in the transcripts made by the Reverend A. B. Nicholls.

C5

Lines by A.G.A. to A.S.　　　　May 20, 1838

　　　O wander not so far away
Line　6　Sweet flowers are fresh and grass is green
　　　9　Our woods, even now their young leaves hide
　　10　The blackbird and the throstle well
　　18　The grave shall close those limbs around

Manuscript C5 is cancelled by lines drawn across it.

C6

62.　　　　SONG TO A.A.　　　　May, 1838

This shall be thy lullaby
Rocking on the stormy sea,
Though it roar in thunder wild
Sleep, stilly sleep, my dark haired child.

[1] This word is "Can" in the manuscript.

When our shuddering boat was crossing
Elderno lake so rudely tossing *
Then 'twas first my nursling smiled;
Sleep, softly sleep, my fair browed child.

Waves above thy cradle break,
Foamy tears are on thy cheek
Yet the Ocean's self grows mild
When it bears my slumbering child.

D6

SONG   May, 1838   Blanche

This shall be thy lullaby
Line 4 Sleep, stilly sleep, thou bright haired child
     5 When our shivering boat was crossing *
     8 Sleep, softly sleep, thou Fairbrowed child *
   12 When it clasps my slumbering child *

Manuscript D6 is cancelled by lines drawn across it.

B11

63.   GLENEDEN'S DREAM   E.   May 21, 1838

Tell me, watcher, is it winter? *
Say how long my sleep has been?
Have the woods I left so lovely
Lost their robes of tender green?

Is the morning slow in coming?
Is the night-time loath to go?
Tell me, are the dreary mountains
Drearier still with drifted snow?

"Captive, since thou sawest the forest,
10 All its leaves have died away,

And another March has woven
Garlands for another May.

"Ice has barred the Arctic water,*
Soft south winds have set it free; *
And once more to deep green valley
Golden flowers might welcome thee."

Watcher, in this lonely prison,
Shut from joy and kindly air,
Heaven, descending in a vision,
20 Taught my soul to do and bear.

It was night, a night in winter;
I lay on the dungeon floor,
And all other sounds were silent—
All, except the river's roar.

Over Death and Desolation,
Fireless hearths and lifeless homes;
Over orphans' heart-sick sorrows,
Over fathers' bloody tombs;

Over friends, that my arms never
30 Might embrace in love again—
Memory pondered, until madness
Struck its poignard in my brain.*

Deepest slumber followed raving,*
Yet, methought, I brooded still;
Still I saw my country bleeding,
Dying for a Tyrant's will—

Not because *my* bliss was blasted,
Burned within, the avenging flame;
Not because my scattered kindred
40 Died in woe or lived in shame.

God doth know, I would have given
Every bosom dear to me,
Could that sacrifice have purchased
Tortured Gondal's liberty!

But, that at Ambition's bidding
All her cherished hopes should wane;
That her noblest sons should muster,
Strive and fight, and fall in vain—

Hut and castle, hall and cottage,
50 Roofless, crumbling to the ground—
Mighty Heaven, a glad Avenger
Thy eternal justice found!

Yes, the arm that once would shudder
Even to pierce a wounded deer,*
I beheld it, unrelenting,
Choke in blood it's sovereign's prayer.

Glorious dream! I saw the city
Blazing in imperial shine;
And among adoring thousands
60 Stood a man of form divine.

None need point the princely victim—
Now he smiles with royal pride!
Now his glance is bright as lightning;
Now—the knife is in his side!

Ha, I saw how death could darken—
Darken that triumphant eye!
His red heart's blood drenched my dagger;
My ear drank his dying sigh!

Shadows come! What means this midnight?
70 O my God, I know it all!
Know the fever-dream is over!
Unavenged the Avengers fall!

J289

June, 1838

None of my kindred now can tell
The features once beloved so well:
Those dark brown locks that used to deck
A snowy brow in ringlets small,
Now wildly shade my sunburnt neck,
And streaming down my shoulders fall.

The pure bright red of noble birth
Has deepened to a gipsy glow;
And care has quenched the smile of mirth,
And tuned my heart to welcome woe.

Yet you must know in infancy
Full many an eye watched over me;
Sweet voices to my slumber sung;
My downy couch with silk was hung;

And music soothed me when I cried;
And when I laughed they all replied;
And "rosy Blanche"—how oft was heard
In hall and bower that well-known word.

Through gathering summers still caressed;
In kingly courts a favourite guest,
A monarch's hand would pour for me
The richest gifts of royalty.

But clouds will come; too soon they came;
For not through age and not through crime,
Is Blanche a now forgotten name;
True heart, and brow unmarked by time:
These treasured blessings still are mine.

Dɪo

65.

'Twas one of those dark, cloudy days
That sometimes come in summer's blaze,
When heaven drops not, when earth is still,
And deeper green is on the hill.

———

66. Lonely at her window sitting,
While the evening stole away; *
Fitful winds, foreboding, flitting
Through a sky of cloudy grey.

———

67. There are two trees in a lonely field;
They breathe a spell to me;
A dreary thought their dark boughs yield,
All waving solemnly.

———

68. What is that smoke that ever still
Comes rolling down that dark brown hill? *

———

69. Still as she looked the iron clouds *
Would part, and sunlight shone between,
But drearily strange and pale and cold.

———

70. Away, away, resign me now *
To scenes of gloom and thoughts of fear;
I trace the signal on thy brow,*
Welcome at last, though once so drear.

———

71. It will not shine again;
    Its sad course is done;
    I have seen the last ray wane
    Of the cold, bright sun.

---

72. None but one beheld him dying,
    Parting with the parting day;
    Winds of evening, sadly sighing,
    Bore his soul from earth away.

---

73. Coldly, bleakly, drearily,
    Evening died on Elbë's shore;
    Winds were in the cloudy sky,
    Sighing, mourning evermore.

---

74. Old Hall of Elbë, ruined, lonely now;
    House to which the voice of life shall never more return; *
    Chambers roofless, desolate, where weeds and ivy grow;
    Windows through whose broken arches the night-winds sadly
        mourn; *
    Home of the departed, the long-departed dead.

B9

75.   DOUGLAS'S RIDE   July 11, 1838

    Well, narrower draw the circle round,
    And hush that organ's solemn sound; *
    And quench the lamp, and stir the fire
    To rouse its flickering radiance higher;
    Loop up the window's velvet veil
    That we may hear the night-wind wail;
    For wild those gusts, and well their chimes
    Blend with a song of troubled times—

SONG

What rider up Gobelrin's glen *
10 Has spurred his straining steed,
And fast and far from living men
Has pressed with maddening speed? *

I saw his hoof-prints mark the rock
When swift he left the plain;
I heard deep down the echoing shock
Re-echo back again.

From cliff to cliff, through rock and heath,
That coal-black courser bounds;
Nor heeds the river pent beneath,
20 Nor marks how fierce it sounds.

With streaming hair and forehead bare
And mantle waving wide,
His master rides; the eagles there
Soar up on every side;

The goats fly by with timid cry,
Their realm so rashly won,*
They pause—he still ascends on high;
They gaze—but he is gone.

O gallant horse, hold on thy course!
30 The road is tracked behind—
Spur, rider, spur, or vain thy force;
Death comes on every wind.

Roared thunder loud from that pitchy cloud?
From it the torrents flow;
Or, woke the breeze in the swaying trees *
That frown so dark below?

He breathes at last, when the valley is past;
He rests on the grey rock's brow—
What ails thee, steed? At thy master's need,
40 Wilt thou prove faithless now?

No; hardly checked, with ears erect,
The charger champed his rein,
Ere his quivering limbs, all foam-beflecked,
Were off like light again.

Hark; through the pass, with threatening crash,
Comes on the increasing roar!
But what shall brave the deep, deep wave—
The deadly path before? *

Their feet are dyed in a darker tide
50 Who dare those dangers drear;
Their breasts have burst through the battle's worst,
And why should they tremble here?

Strong hearts they bear, and arms as good,
To conquer or to fall;
They dash into the boiling flood,
They gain the rock's steep wall—

"Now, my bold men, this one pass more,*
This narrow chasm of stone,
And Douglas, for our sovereign's gore,
60 Shall yield us back his own."

I hear their ever-nearing tread *
Sound through the granite glen;
There is a tall pine overhead
Laid by the mountain men.*

That dizzy bridge, which no horse could track,
Has choked the outlaw's way; *
There, like a wild beast, he turns back,*
And grimly stands at bay.

Why smiles he so, when far below
70 He sees the toiling chase? *
The ponderous tree sways heavily
And totters from its place.

They raise their eyes, for the sunny skies
Are lost in sudden shade;
But, Douglas neither shrinks nor flies—
He need not fly the dead.

B16

76.   A.G.A.   E.   August 30, 1838

For him who struck thy foreign string,
I ween this heart hath ceased to care; *
Then why dost thou such feelings bring
To my sad spirit, old guitar?

It is as if the warm sunlight
In some deep glen should lingering stay,
When clouds of tempest and of night *
Had wrapt the parent orb away.*

It is as if the glassy brook
Should image still its willows fair,
Though years ago the woodman's stroke
Laid low in dust their gleaming hair.*

Even so, guitar, thy magic tone
Has moved the tear and waked the sigh,*
Has bid the ancient torrent flow *
Although its very source is dry!

Above this poem in the manuscript Charlotte Brontë has written, "The Lady to her guitar."

H485

THE LADY TO HER GUITAR

For him who struck thy foreign string
Line 2 I ween this heart has ceased to care
     7 When clouds of storm, or shades of night
     8 Have wrapt the parent orb away
   12 Laid low in dust their Dryad-hair
   14 Hath moved the tear, and waked the sigh
   15 Hath bid the ancient torrent moan

E12

77.   Arthr Ex [1]
                                    To ——

In dungeons dark I cannot sing,
In sorrow's thrall 'tis hard to smile:
What bird can soar with broken wing?
What heart can bleed and joy the while?

78.   September 23, 1838

The evening sun was sinking down
On low green hills and clustered trees;
It was a scene as fair and lone
As ever felt the soothing breeze

That bends the grass, when day is gone,*
And gives the wave a brighter blue,*
And makes the soft white clouds sail on
Like spirits of ethereal dew

  [1] Probably meant for "Arthur Exina." The name "Marcius" is written in pencil
below the dash in the manuscript.

Which all the morn had hovered o'er
The azure flowers where they were nursed,
And now return to heaven once more
Where their bright glories shone at first.

* * A * * A * * *

79.   Fall, leaves, fall; die, flowers, away;
Lengthen night and shorten day;
Every leaf speaks bliss to me
Fluttering from the autumn tree.
I shall smile when wreaths of snow
Blossom where the rose should grow;
I shall sing when night's decay
Ushers in a drearier day.

* * A * A * * *

Manuscript E12 is a separate leaf, containing Nos. 87, 88, an early draft
of 90, and 89 on one side; and on the reverse Nos. 77, 78, 79, and the first
10 lines of No. 91, respectively.

B13

80.   E.   October 17, 1838
SONG BY JULIUS BRENZAIDA
TO G.S.

Geraldine, the moon is shining
With so soft, so bright a ray;
Seems it not that eve, declining,*
Ushered in a fairer day?

While the wind is whispering only,
Far—across the water borne,*
Let us in this silence lonely
Sit beneath the ancient thorn.

Wild the road, and rough and dreary;
Barren all the moorland round;

Rude the couch that rests us weary;
Mossy stone and heathy ground.

But, when winter storms were meeting
In the moonless, midnight dome,
Did we heed the tempest's beating,
Howling round our spirits' home?

No; that tree with branches riven,
Whitening in the whirl of snow,
As it tossed against the heaven,
Sheltered happy hearts below—

And at Autumn's mild returning
Shall our feet forget the way?
And in Cynthia's silver morning,
Geraldine, wilt thou delay?

B14

81.   E.   October 17, 1838
SONG BY J. BRENZAIDA
TO G.S.

I knew not 'twas so dire a crime
To say the word, Adieu;
But this shall be the only time
My slighted heart shall sue.*

The wild moorside, the winter morn,*
The gnarled and ancient tree—
If in your breast they waken scorn,
Shall wake the same in me.

I can forget black eyes and brows,
And lips of rosy charm,*
If you forget the sacred vows
Those faithless lips could form.

If hard commands can tame your love,
Or prison walls can hold,*
I would not wish to grieve above
A thing so false and cold.

And there are bosoms bound to mine
With links both tried and strong;
And there are eyes whose lightning shine
Has warmed and blessed me long:

Those eyes shall make my only day,
Shall set my spirit free,
And chase the foolish thoughts away
That mourn your memory!

Under the heading to this poem in the manuscript Charlotte Brontë
has written "Love's Farewell."

H484

LAST WORDS

I knew not 'twas so dire a crime
Line 4 My lips or heart shall sue
       5 The wild hill-side, the winter morn
      10 And lips of falsest charm
      14 Or strongest walls can hold

Dii

82.   October, 1838
                                             A.G.A.

Where were ye all? and where wert thou?
I saw an eye that shone like thine;
But dark curls waved around his brow,
And his stern glance was strange to mine.

And yet a dreamlike comfort came
Into my heart and anxious eye;
And, trembling yet to hear his name,
I bent to listen watchfully.

His voice, though never heard before,*
Still spoke to me of years gone by;
It seemed a vision to restore
That brought the hot tears to my eye.

———

83. I paused on the threshold, I turned to the sky;
I looked on the heaven and the dark mountains round; *
The full moon sailed bright through that Ocean on high,
And the wind murmured past with a wild eerie sound;

And I entered the walls of my dark prison-house;
Mysterious it rose from the billowy moor.

*   *   *   *   *

84.   O come with me, thus ran the song,
The moon is bright in Autumn's sky,
And thou hast toiled and laboured long
With aching head and weary eye.

———

B18

85. F. DE SAMARA TO A.G.A.   E.   November 1, 1838

Light up thy halls! 'Tis closing day;
I'm drear and lone and far away—
Cold blows on my breast the northwind's bitter sigh,
And oh, my couch is bleak beneath the rainy sky!

Light up thy halls—and think not of me; *
That face is absent now, thou hast hated so to see—*

Bright be thine eyes, undimmed their dazzling shine,
For never, never more shall they encounter mine!

The desert moor is dark; there is tempest in the air;
I have breathed my only wish in one last, one burning prayer—
A prayer that would come forth, although it lingered long;
That set on fire my heart, but froze upon my tongue.

And now, it shall be done before the morning rise:
I will not watch the sun ascend in yonder skies.*
One task alone remains—thy pictured face to view;
And then I go to prove if God, at least, be true!

Do I not see thee now? Thy black resplendent hair;
Thy glory-beaming brow, and smile, how heavenly fair!
Thine eyes are turned away—those eyes I would not see;
Their dark, their deadly ray, would more than madden me.

There, go, Deceiver, go! My hand is streaming wet; *
My heart's blood flows to buy the blessing— To forget!
Oh could that lost heart give back, back again to thine,*
One tenth part of the pain that clouds my dark decline!

Oh could I see thy lids weighed down in cheerless woe;
Too full to hide their tears, too stern to overflow;
Oh could I know thy soul with equal grief was torn,
This fate might be endured—this anguish might be borne!

How gloomy grows the night! 'Tis Gondal's wind that blows;
I shall not tread again the deep glens where it rose—
I feel it on my face— "Where, wild blast, dost thou roam?
What do we, wanderer, here, so far away from home?

"I do not need thy breath to cool my death-cold brow;
But go to that far land, where she is shining now;

Tell Her my latest wish, tell Her my dreary doom;
Say that *my* pangs are past, but *Hers* are yet to come."

Vain words—vain, frenzied thoughts! No ear can hear me
   call—*
Lost in the vacant air my frantic curses fall—*
And could she see me now, perchance her lip would smile,
Would smile in careless pride and utter scorn the while!

And yet for all her hate, each parting glance would tell *
A stronger passion breathed, burned, in this last farewell.
Unconquered in my soul the Tyrant rules me still;
Life bows to my control, but *Love* I cannot kill!

A12

86.   November 5, 1838

   O Dream, where art thou now?
   Long years have past away
   Since last, from off thine angel brow
   I saw the light decay.

   Alas, alas for me
   Thou wert so bright and fair,
   I could not think thy memory
   Would yield me nought but care!

   The sun-beam and the storm,
   The summer-eve divine,
   The silent night of solemn calm,
   The full moon's cloudless shine,

   Were once entwined with thee,
   But now with weary pain,
   Lost vision! 'tis enough for me—
   Thou canst not shine again.

C10

November 5, 1838

O Dream, where art thou now?
Line 3 Since last from off thy angel brow

Only the first three verses are in this manuscript. They have been cancelled by lines drawn lightly across them.

E12

87.   When days of Beauty deck the earth *
       Or stormy nights descend,
       How well my spirit knows the path
       On which it ought to wend.

       It seeks the consecrated spot
       Beloved in childhood's years,
       The space between is all forgot
       Its sufferings and its tears.

       * * * * * *

88.   Still beside that dreary water
       Stood he 'neath the cold moon ray *
       Thinking on the deed of slaughter
       On his heart that darkly lay.

       Soft the voice that broke his dreaming
       Stealing through the silent air;
       Yet, before, the raven's screaming
       He had heard regardless there.

       Once his name was sweetly uttered,
       Then the echo died away,

But each pulse in horror fluttered
As the life would pass away.

Following the above in the manuscript is a crude sketch of distant
hills, with the rising or setting sun. This is followed by 8 lines, apparently an early draft of No. 90.

89.　　There swept adown that dreary glen
　　　A wilder sound than mountain wind:
　　　The thrilling shouts of fighting men
　　　With something sadder far behind.

　　　The thrilling shouts they died away
　　　Before the night came greyly down;
　　　But closed not with the closing day
　　　The choking sob, the tortured moan.

　　　Down in a hollow sunk in shade
　　　Where dark heath waved in secret gloom,*
　　　A weary bleeding form was laid *
　　　Waiting the death that was to come.

J285

90.　　The starry night shall tidings bring:
　　　Go out upon the breezy moor,
　　　Watch for a bird with sable wing,
　　　And beak and talons dropping gore.

　　　Look not around, look not beneath,
　　　But mutely trace its airy way;
　　　Mark where it lights upon the heath,
　　　Then wanderer kneel thee down and pray.

　　　What fortune may await thee there
　　　I will not and I dare not tell,
　　　But Heaven is moved by fervent prayer
　　　And God is mercy—fare thee well!

E12

Nov., 1838

The starry night shall comfort bring:
Go out upon the breezy moor,
Watch for a bird with sable wing
And beak and talons dropping gore.

It will perch on a heathy swell,
Against the light of the coming moon;
Then, poor wretch, thy misery tell:
Thou shalt have the wished-for boon.

* * * * *

These two verses are cancelled in the manuscript. The second verse
is now printed for the first time.

A1

91. November 11, 1838

Loud without the wind was roaring
   Through the waned autumnal sky;
Drenching wet, the cold rain pouring
   Spoke of stormy winters nigh.

   All too like that dreary eve
   Sighed within repining grief;
   Sighed at first, but sighed not long—
   Sweet—How softly sweet it came!
   Wild words of an ancient song,
10   Undefined, without a name.

"It was spring, for the skylark was singing."
   Those words, they awakened a spell—

They unlocked a deep fountain whose springing
Nor Absence nor Distance can quell.

In the gloom of a cloudy November,
They uttered the music of May;
They kindled the perishing ember
Into fervour that could not decay.

Awaken on all my dear moorlands
20 The wind in its glory and pride!
O call me from valleys and highlands
To walk by the hill-river's side!

It is swelled with the first snowy weather;
The rocks they are icy and hoar
And darker waves round the long heather
And the fern-leaves are sunny no more.

There are no yellow-stars on the mountain,
The blue-bells have long died away
From the brink of the moss-bedded fountain,
30 From the side of the wintery brae—

But lovelier than corn-fields all waving
In emerald and scarlet and gold
Are the slopes where the north-wind is raving,
And the glens where I wandered of old.

"It was morning; the bright sun was beaming."
How sweetly that brought back to me
The time when nor labour nor dreaming
Broke the sleep of the happy and free.

But blithely we rose as the dusk heaven
40 Was melting to amber and blue;
And swift were the wings to our feet given
While we traversed the meadows of dew,

For the moors, for the moors where the short grass
Like velvet beneath us should lie!
For the moors, for the moors where each high pass
Rose sunny against the clear sky!

For the moors where the linnet was trilling
Its song on the old granite stone;
Where the lark—the wild skylark was filling
50   Every breast with delight like its own.

What language can utter the feeling
That rose when, in exile afar,
On the brow of a lonely hill kneeling
I saw the brown heath growing there.

It was scattered and stunted, and told me
That soon even that would be gone;
Its whispered, "The grim walls enfold me;
I have bloomed in my last summer's sun."

But not the loved music whose waking
60   Makes the soul of the Swiss die away
Has a spell more adored and heart-breaking
Than in its half-blighted bells lay.

The spirit that bent 'neath its power,
How it longed, how it burned to be free!
If I could have wept in that hour
Those tears had been heaven to me.

Well, well, the sad minutes are moving
Though loaded with trouble and pain;
And sometime the loved and the loving
70   Shall meet on the mountains again.

E12

November, 1838

Loud without the wind was roaring
Line 6 Sighed without repining grief

Only the first 10 lines are in this manuscript. See page 82.
Charlotte Brontë made many alterations in this poem when she prepared it for printing in 1850:

H476

STANZAS

Loud without the wind was roaring
Line 2 Through th'autumnal sky
     4 Spoke of winter nigh
     6 Did my exiled spirit grieve
     7 Grieved at first, but grieved not long
   11 "It was spring, and the skylark was singing"
   19 Awaken, o'er all my dear moorland
   20 West wind, in thy glory and pride
   21 Oh! call me from valley and lowland
   22 To walk by the hill-torrent's side
   25 And sullenly waves the long heather
   32 In emerald, and vermeil, and gold
   33 Are the heights where the north wind is raving
   34 And the crags where I wandered of old
   36 How sweetly it brought back to me
   39 But blithely we rose as the dawn-heaven
   42 As we traversed the meadows of dew
   52 Which rose, when in exile afar
   62 Than, for me, in that blighted heath lay
   63 The spirit, which bent 'neath its power

A2

92.

December 4, 1838

A little while, a little while,
The noisy crowd are barred away;

And I can sing and I can smile
A little while I've holyday!

Where wilt thou go, my harassed heart?
Full many a land invites thee now;
And places near and far apart
Have rest for thee, my weary brow.

There is a spot 'mid barren hills
Where winter howls and driving rain,
But if the dreary tempest chills
There is a light that warms again.

The house is old, the trees are bare
And moonless bends the misty dome
But what on earth is half so dear,
So longed for as the hearth of home?

The mute bird sitting on the stone,
The dank moss dripping from the wall,
The garden-walk with weeds o'ergrown,
I love them—how I love them all!

Shall I go there? or shall I seek
Another clime, another sky,
Where tongues familiar music speak
In accents dear to memory? *

Yes, as I mused, the naked room,
The flickering firelight died away
And from the midst of cheerless gloom
I passed to bright, unclouded day—

A little and a lone green lane
That opened on a common wide;
A distant, dreamy, dim blue chain
Of mountains circling every side;

A heaven so clear, an earth so calm,
So sweet, so soft, so hushed an air
And, deepening still the dream-like charm,
Wild moor-sheep feeding everywhere—

That was the scene; I knew it well,
I knew the path-ways far and near
That winding o'er each billowy swell
Marked out the tracks of wandering deer.

Could I have lingered but an hour
It well had paid a week of toil,
But truth has banished fancy's power;
I hear my dungeon bars recoil—

Even as I stood with raptured eye
Absorbed in bliss so deep and dear
My hour of rest had fleeted by
And given me back to weary care.

In the manuscript, the words "A little," in line 4 are not written clearly, and were read by Charlotte Brontë as "Alike" when she prepared the poem for publication in 1850. She made many other alterations, most of which are interlined, in pencil, in her handwriting.

H474

STANZAS

A little while, a little while
Line 2 The weary task is put away
    4 Alike, while I have holiday
    6 What thought, what scene invites thee now?
    7 What spot, or near or far apart
    8 Has rest for thee, my weary brow?
  14 Moonless above bends twilight's dome
  19 The thorn-trees gaunt, the walks o'ergrown
Lines 21 to 24 were omitted by Charlotte Brontë.
Line 25 Still, as I mused, the naked room,

26 The alien firelight died away
38 I knew the turfy pathway's sweep
40 Marked out the tracks of wandering sheep
44 Restraint and heavy task recoil
48 And back came labour, bondage, care.

A3

93.   December 7, 1838

How still, how happy! Those are words *
That once would scarce agree together;
I loved the plashing of the surge,
The changing heaven, the breezy weather,

More than smooth seas and cloudless skies
And solemn, soothing, softened airs
That in the forest woke no sighs
And from the green spray shook no tears.

How still, how happy! Now I feel
Where silence dwells is sweeter far
Than laughing mirth's most joyous swell
However pure its raptures are.

Come, sit down on this sunny stone:
'Tis wintry light o'er flowerless moors—
But sit—for we are all alone
And clear expand heaven's breathless shores.

I could think in the withered grass
Spring's budding wreaths we might discern;
The violet's eye might shyly flash
And young leaves shoot among the fern.

It is but thought—full many a night
The snow shall clothe those hills afar

And storms shall add a drearier blight
And winds shall wage a wilder war,

Before the lark may herald in
Fresh foliage twined with blossoms fair
And summer days again begin
Their glory-haloed crown to wear.

Yet my heart loves December's smile
As much as July's golden beam;
Then let us sit and watch the while *
The blue ice curdling on the stream.

A4

94.   December 18, 1838

The blue bell is the sweetest flower
That waves in summer air;
Its blossoms have the mightiest power
To soothe my spirit's care.

There is a spell in purple heath
Too wildly, sadly dear;
The violet has a fragrant breath
But fragrance will not cheer.

The trees are bare, the sun is cold,
And seldom, seldom seen;
The heavens have lost their zone of gold
The earth its robe of green;

And ice upon the glancing stream
Has cast its sombre shade
And distant hills and valleys seem
In frozen mist arrayed.

The blue bell cannot charm me now,
The heath has lost its bloom,
The violets in the glen below
They yield no sweet perfume.

But though I mourn the heather-bell
'Tis better far, away;
I know how fast my tears would swell
To see it smile to-day;

And that wood flower that hides so shy
Beneath its [1] mossy stone *
Its balmy scent and dewy eye:
'Tis not for them I moan.

It is the slight and stately stem,
The blossoms silvery blue,
The buds hid like a sapphire gem
In sheaths of emerald hue.*

'Tis these that breathe upon my heart
A calm and softening spell
That if it makes the tear-drop start
Has power to soothe as well.

For these I weep, so long divided
Through winter's dreary day,
In longing weep—but most when guided
On withered banks to stray.

If chilly then the light should fall
Adown the dreary sky
And gild the dank and darkened wall
With transient brilliancy,

[1] In the manuscript the word "the" has been overwritten to read "its," or vice versa.

How do I yearn, how do I pine
For the time of flowers to come,
And turn me from that fading shine
To mourn the fields of home.

As printed by Charlotte Brontë in 1850, the poem contains several differences, and four of the stanzas were omitted:

H475

THE BLUEBELL

The Bluebell is the sweetest flower
Line 12 And earth her robe of green
    21 But though I mourn the sweet Bluebell
Lines 25 to 40 were omitted.
Line 41 For, oh! when chill the sunbeams fall
    42 Adown that dreary sky,
    43 And gild yon dank and darkened wall
    45 How do I weep, how do I pine

D7

95.   January 12, 1839

The night was dark, yet winter breathed
With softened sighs on Gondal's shore;
And, though its wind repining grieved,
It chained the snow-swollen streams no more.

How deep into the wilderness
My horse had strayed, I cannot say;
But neither morsel nor caress
Would urge him farther on the way;

So, loosening from his neck the rein,
10 I set my worn companion free;
And billowy hill and boundless plain
Full soon divided him from me.

The sullen clouds lay all unbroken
And blackening round the horizon drear;
But still they gave no certain token
Of heavy rain or tempests near.*

I paused, confounded and distressed;
Down in the heath my limbs I threw;
Yet wilder as I longed for rest
20 More wakeful heart and eyelids grew.

It was about the middle night,
And under such a starless dome
When, gliding from the mountain's height,
I saw a shadowy spirit come.

Her wavy hair, on her shoulders bare,
It shone like soft clouds round the moon;
Her noiseless feet, like melting sleet,
Gleamed white a moment, then were gone.

"What seek you now, on this bleak moor's brow?
30 Where wanders that form from heaven descending?"
It was thus I said as, her graceful head,
The spirit above my couch was bending.

"This is my home, where whirlwinds blow,
Where snowdrifts round my path are swelling;
'Tis many a year, 'tis long ago,
Since I beheld another dwelling.

"When thick and fast the smothering blast
O'erwhelmed the hunter on the plain,
If my cheek grew pale in its loudest gale
40 May I never tread the hills again.

"The shepherd had died on the mountain side,
But my ready aid was near him then:

I led him back o'er the hidden track,
And gave him to his native glen.

"When tempests roar on the lonely shore,
I light my beacon with sea-weeds dry,
And it flings its fire through the darkness dire
And gladdens the sailor's hopeless eye.

"And the scattered sheep, I love to keep *
50 Their timid forms to guard from harm;
I have a spell, and they know it well,
And I save them with a powerful charm.

"Thy own good steed on his friendless bed
A few hours since you left to die;
But I knelt by his side and the saddle untied,
And life returned to his glazing eye.

"And deem thou not that quite forgot
My mercy will forsake me now: *
I bring thee care and not despair;
60 Abasement but not overthrow.

"To a silent home thy foot may come *
And years may follow of toilsome pain;
But yet I swear by that burning tear
The loved shall meet on its hearth again."

E5

96.　A.G.A.　　　　　　　　　　　March 27, 1839

What winter floods, what showers of spring *
Have drenched the grass by night and day;
And yet, beneath, that spectre ring,*
Unmoved and undiscovered lay

A mute remembrancer of crime,*
Long lost, concealed, forgot for years,
It comes at last to cancel time,
And waken unavailing tears.

BIO

97.   BY R. GLENEDEN   E.   April 17, 1839

From our evening fireside now,
Merry laugh and cheerful tone,
Smiling eye and cloudless brow,
Mirth and music, all are flown;

Yet the grass before the door
Grows as green in April rain;
And as blithely as of yore
Larks have poured their day-long strain.

Is it fear or is it sorrow
Checks the stagnant stream of joy? *
Do we tremble that to-morrow
May our present peace destroy?

For past misery are we weeping?
What is past can hurt no more;
And the gracious heavens are keeping
Aid for that which lies before.

One is absent, and for one
Cheerless, chill is our hearthstone.
One is absent, and for him
Cheeks are pale and eyes are dim.

Arthur, brother, Gondal's shore
Rested from the battle's roar—
Arthur, brother, we returned
Back to Desmond lost and mourned.

Thou didst purchase by thy fall
Home for us and peace for all;
Yet, how darkly dawned that day—
Dreadful was the price to pay!

Just as once, through sun and mist
I have climbed the mountain's breast,
Still my gun, with certain aim,
Brought to earth the fluttering game;

But the very dogs repined;
Though I called with whistle shrill,
Listlessly they lagged behind,
Looking backward o'er the hill.

Sorrow was not vocal there:
Mute their pain and my despair;
But the joy of life was flown:
He was gone and we were lone.

So it is by morn and eve—
So it is in field and hall:
For the absent one we grieve,
One being absent saddens All.

In the transcript of this poem, made by the Reverend A. B. Nicholls, the heading has been replaced by the title "The Absent One."

C13

LINES BY R.G.   April 17, 1839

From our evening fireside now
Line 35 Tay and Carlo lagged behind
38 Mute their woe and my despair

This manuscript, cancelled by lines drawn across it, contains only lines 1 to 3 and 34 to 44, lines 4 to 33 having been on a separate leaf, which is missing.

C4

98.   SONG   April 20, 1839

King Julius left the south country
His banners all bravely flying;
His followers went out with Jubilee
But they shall return with sighing.

Loud arose the triumphal hymn
The drums were loudly rolling,
Yet you might have heard in distance dim
How a passing bell was tolling.

The sword so bright from battles won
With unseen rust is fretting,
The evening comes before the noon,
The scarce risen sun is setting.

While princes hang upon his breath
And nations round are fearing,
Close by his side a daggered death
With sheathless point stands sneering.

That death he took a certain aim,
For Death is stony-hearted
And in the zenith of his fame
Both power and life departed.

C16

99.   LINES   April 28, 1839

The soft unclouded blue of air,
The earth as golden-green and fair
And bright as Eden's used to be:
That air and earth have rested me.

Laid on the grass I lapsed away,
Sank back again to childhood's day;
All harsh thoughts perished, memory mild
Subdued both grief and passion wild.

But did the sunshine even now
10 That bathed his stern and swarthy brow,
Oh, did it wake—I long to know—
One whisper, one sweet dream in him,
One lingering joy that years ago
Had faded—lost in distance dim?

That iron man was born like me,
And he was once an ardent boy:
He must have felt, in infancy,
The glory of a summer sky.

Though storms untold his mind have tossed,
20 He cannot utterly have lost
Remembrance of his early home—
So lost that not a gleam may come;

No vision of his mother's face
When she so fondly would set free *
Her darling child from her embrace
To roam till eve at liberty:

Nor of his haunts, nor of the flowers
His tiny hand would grateful bear
Returning from the darkening bowers,
30 To weave into her glossy hair.

I saw the light breeze kiss his cheek,
His fingers 'mid the roses twined;
I watched to mark one transient streak
Of pensive softness shade his mind.

The open window showed around
A glowing park and glorious sky,
And thick woods swelling with the sound
Of Nature's mingled harmony.

Silent he sat. That stormy breast
40 At length, I said, has deigned to rest;
At length above that spirit flows
The waveless ocean of repose.

Let me draw near: 'twill soothe to view
His dark eyes dimmed with holy dew;
Remorse even now may wake within,
And half unchain his soul from sin.

Perhaps this is the destined hour
When hell shall lose its fatal power
And heaven itself shall bend above
50 To hail the soul redeemed by love.

Unmarked I gazed; my idle thought
Passed with the ray whose shine it caught;
One glance revealed how little care
He felt for all the beauty there.

Oh, crime can make the heart grow old
Sooner than years of wearing woe;
Can turn the warmest bosom cold
As winter wind or polar snow.

B7

100. A.G.A.   TO THE BLUEBELL   E.   May 9, 1839

Sacred watcher, wave thy bells!
Fair hill flower and woodland child!
Dear to me in deep green dells—
Dearest on the mountains wild.

Bluebell, even as all divine
I have seen my darling shine—
Bluebell, even as wan and frail
I have seen my darling fail—
Thou hast found a voice for me,
And soothing words are breathed by thee.

Thus they murmur, "Summer's sun
Warms me till my life is done.
Would I rather choose to die
Under winter's ruthless sky?

"Glad I bloom and calm I fade;
Weeping twilight dews my bed;
Mourner, mourner, dry thy tears—
Sorrow comes with lengthened years!"

C7

TO A BLUEBELL

by A.G.A.   May 9, 1839

    Sacred watcher, wave thy bells
Line 9 Lift thy head and speak to me
   10 Soothing thoughts are breathed by thee
   11 Thus they whisper, "Summer's sun
   12 Lights my course commenced and done [or] *
       Lights me till my life is done
   14 Under Winter's stormy sky
   16 Dews of heaven are round me shed *

This manuscript has been cancelled by lines drawn across it.

E1

101.   May 25, 1839

May flowers are opening
And leaves unfolding free;

There are bees in every blossom
And birds on every tree.

The sun is gladly shining,
The stream sings merrily,
And I only am pining *
And all is dark to me.

O cold, cold is my heart!
It will not, cannot rise;
It feels no sympathy
With those refulgent skies.

Dead, dead is my joy,
I long to be at rest;
I wish the damp earth covered
This desolate breast.*

If I were quite alone,
It might not be so drear,
When all hope was gone;
At least I could not fear.

But the glad eyes around me
Must weep as mine have done,
And I must see the same gloom *
Eclipse their morning sun.

If heaven would rain on me
That future storm of care,
So their fond hearts were free
I'd be content to bear.

Alas! as lightning withers
The young and agèd tree,
Both they and I shall fall beneath
The fate we cannot flee.
                    E. J. Brontë

C14

LINES BY CLAUDIA May 28, 1839

I did not sleep; 'twas noon of day,
I saw the burning sunshine fall,
The long grass bending where I lay,
The blue sky brooding over all.

I heard the mellow hum of bees
And singing birds and sighing trees,
And far away in woody dell
The Music of the Sabbath bell.

I did not dream; remembrance still
Clasped round my heart its fetters chill;
But I am sure the soul is free
To leave its clay a little while,
Or how in exile misery
Could I have seen my country smile?

In English fields my limbs were laid
With English turf beneath my head;
My spirit wandered o'er that shore
Where nought but it may wander more.

Yet if the soul can thus return
I need not and I will not mourn;
And vainly did you drive me far
With leagues of ocean stretched between:
My mortal flesh you might debar,
But not the eternal fire within.

My Monarch died to rule forever
A heart that can forget him never;
And dear to me, aye, doubly dear,

Though shut within the silent tomb,
His name shall be for whom I bear
This long-sustained and hopeless doom.

And brighter in the hour of woe
Than in the blaze of victory's pride,
That glory shedding star shall glow
For which we fought and bled and died.

E14

103.   June 8, 1839

I know not how it falls on me,
This summer evening, hushed and lone;
Yet the faint wind comes soothingly
With something of an olden tone.

Forgive me if I've shunned so long
Your gentle greeting, earth and air!
But sorrow withers even the strong,*
And who can fight against despair?

B19

104.   E.J.   June 14, 1839
WRITTEN ON RETURNING TO THE P. OF I.[1]
ON THE 10th of JANUARY, 1827

The busy day has hurried by,
And hearts greet kindred hearts once more;
And swift the evening hours should fly,
But—what turns every gleaming eye
So often to the door,

And then so quick away—and why
Does sudden silence chill the room,

[1] Palace of Instruction (see page 167).

And laughter sink into a sigh,
And merry words to whispers die,
And gladness change to gloom?

O we are listening for a sound
We know shall ne'er be heard again;
Sweet voices in the halls resound,
Fair forms, fond faces gather round,
But all in vain—in vain!

Their feet shall never waken more *
The echoes in these galleries wide,
Nor dare the snow on the mountain's brow,*
Nor skim the river's frozen flow,
Nor wander down its side.

They who have been our life—our soul—
Through summer-youth, from childhood's spring—
Who bound us in one vigorous whole
To stand 'gainst Tyranny's control
For ever triumphing—

Who bore the brunt of battle's fray:
The first to fight, the last to fall;
Whose mighty minds, with kindred ray,
Still led the van in Glory's way;
The idol chiefs of all—

They, they are gone! Not for a while
As golden suns at night decline
And even in death our grief beguile *
Foretelling, with a rose-red smile,
How bright the morn will shine.

No; these dark towers are lone and lorn;
This very crowd is vacancy;
And we must watch and wait and mourn

And half look out for their return,
And think their forms we see;

And fancy music in our ear,
Such as their lips could only pour;
And think we feel their presence near,
And start to find they are not here,
And never shall be more!

E14

This manuscript is a fragment torn from the top of a leaf, and contains
on one side No. 103, and on the reverse two beginnings of No. 104:

> The hours of day have glided by,*
> And hearts greet kindred hearts once more;
> And voices murmur cheerily; *
> But what turns every gleaming eye
> So often to the unopened door?

The 5 lines are cancelled by lines drawn across them, and are followed
by the first 6 lines of the complete poem, the only variation being in
line 1:

> The busy day has glided by

J304

105.   June 18, 1839

Month after month, year after year,
My harp has poured a dreary strain;
At length a livelier note shall cheer,
And pleasure tune its chords again.

What though the stars and fair moonlight
Are quenched in morning dull and grey?
They are but tokens of the night,
And *this,* my soul, is day.

E19

106. She dried her tears, and they did smile
To see her cheeks' returning glow;
Nor did discern how all the while
That full heart throbbed to overflow.

With that sweet look and lively tone,
And bright eye shining all the day,
They could not guess, at midnight lone
How she would weep the time away.

D1

107. E. J. Brontë   July 12, 1839

And now the house-dog stretched once more
His limbs upon the glowing floor;
The children half resumed their play,
Though from the warm hearth scared away.
The goodwife left her spinning-wheel,
And spread with smiles the evening meal;
The shepherd placed a seat and pressed
To their poor fare his unknown guest.
And he unclasped his mantle now,
And raised the covering from his brow;
Said, "Voyagers by land and sea
Were seldom feasted daintily";
And checked his host by adding stern *
He'd no refinement to unlearn.
A silence settled on the room;
The cheerful welcome sank to gloom;
But not those words, though cold and high,*
So froze their hospitable joy.
No—there was something in his face,
Some nameless thing they could not trace,

And something in his voice's tone
Which turned their blood as chill as stone.
The ringlets of his long black hair
Fell o'er a cheek most ghastly fair.
Youthful he seemed—but worn as they
Who spend too soon their youthful day.
When his glance drooped, 'twas hard to quell *
Unbidden feelings' sudden swell; *
And pity scarce her tears could hide,
So sweet that brow, with all its pride;
But when upraised his eye would dart
An icy shudder through the heart.
Compassion changed to horror then
And fear to meet that gaze again.
It was not hatred's tiger-glare,
Nor the wild anguish of despair;
It was not useless misery *
Which mocks at friendship's sympathy.
No—lightning all unearthly shone
Deep in that dark eye's circling zone,
Such withering lightning as we deem
None but a spectre's look may beam; *
And glad they were when he turned away
And wrapt him in his mantle grey,
Leant down his head upon his arm *
And veiled from view their[sic] basilisk charm.

B22

108.   A FAREWELL TO ALEXANDRIA   July 12, 1839

I've seen this dell in July's shine
As lovely as an angel's dream;
Above, heaven's depth of blue divine;
Around, the evening's golden beam.

I've seen the purple heather-bell
Look out by many a storm-worn stone;

And oh, I've seen such music swell,
Such wild notes wake these passes lone—

So soft, yet so intensely felt,
So low, yet so distinctly heard,
My breath would pause, my eyes would melt,
And my tears dew the green heath-sward.*

I'd linger here a summer day,
Nor care how fast the hours flew by,
Nor mark the sun's departing ray
Smile sadly glorious from the sky.*

Then, then I might have laid thee down *
And deemed thy sleep would gentle be; *
I might have left thee, darling one,
And thought thy God was guarding thee!

But now there is no wandering glow,
No gleam to say that God is nigh;
And coldly spreads thy couch of snow,*
And harshly sounds thy lullaby.

Forests of heather, dark and long,
Wave their brown, branching arms above,
And they must soothe thee with their song,
And they must shield my child of love!

Alas, the flakes are heavily falling;
They cover fast each guardian crest;
And chilly white their shroud is palling
Thy frozen limbs and freezing breast.

Wakes up the storm more madly wild,
The mountain drifts are tossed on high—
Farewell, unblessed, unfriended child,
I cannot bear to watch thee die!

This poem was given the title of "The Outcast Mother" in *The Corn-hill Magazine,* May, 1860, where it first appeared in print.

D3

Come hither, child—who gifted thee
With power to touch that string so well?
How darest thou rouse up thoughts in me,*
Thoughts that I would, but cannot quell?

Nay, chide not, lady; long ago
I heard those notes in Ula's hall; *
And, had I known they'd waken woe,
I'd weep, their music to recall.

But thus it was: one festal night,
When I was hardly six years old,
I stole away from crowds and light
And sought a chamber dark and cold.

I had no one to love me there;
I knew no comrade and no friend;
And so I went to sorrow where
Heaven, only heaven, saw me bend.*

Loud blew the wind; 'twas sad to stay,
From all that splendour barred away.
I imaged in the lonely room
A thousand forms of fearful gloom; *

And, with my wet eyes raised on high,
I prayed to God that I might die.
Suddenly, in that silence drear,
A sound of music reached my ear;

And then a note; I hear it yet,*
So full of soul, so deeply sweet,

I thought that Gabriel's self had come
To take me to my father's home.

Three times it rose, that seraph-strain,
Then died, nor lived ever again; *
But still the words and still the tone *
Swell round my heart when all alone. *
                Emily Jane Brontë

This poem is written on one side of a single leaf. Alongside it is
written:

                Alas, that she would bid adieu
                To all the hopes her childhood knew.
                Hushed is the harp

On the reverse is the unfinished poem, beginning "I'm standing in the
forest now," No. 110 (D3).

B4

110.   To A.G.A.   E.

"Thou standest in the greenwood now
The place, the hour the same—
And here the fresh leaves gleam and glow
And there, down in the lake below,
The tiny ripples flame.

"The breeze sings like a summer breeze
Should sing in summer skies
And tower-like rocks and tent-like trees
In mingled glory rise.

"But where is he to-day, to-day?"
"O question not with me."
"I will not, Lady; only say
Where may thy lover be?

"Is he upon some distant shore
Or is he on the sea
Or is the heart thou dost adore
A faithless heart to thee?

"The heart I love, whate'er betide,
Is faithful as the grave
And neither foreign lands divide
Nor yet the rolling wave."

"Then why should sorrow cloud that brow
And tears those eyes bedim?
Reply this once—is it that thou
Hast faithless been to him?"

"I gazed upon the cloudless moon
And loved her all the night
Till morning came and ardent noon,
Then I forgot her light—

No—not forgot—eternally
Remains its memory dear;
But could the day seem dark to me
Because the night was fair?

"I well may mourn that only one
Can light my future sky
Even though by such a radiant sun
My moon of life must die."

Now printed for the first time in an edition of the poems; but see note
on p. 35.

This poem appears to be partly a transcript of Manuscripts D3 and D8:

D3

I'm standing in the forest now,
The place, the hour the same;

And here the green leaves gleam [1] and glow,*
And there, down in that lake below,
The tiny ripples flame.

The breeze sings like a summer breeze
Should sing in summer skies;
And tower-like rocks and tent-like trees *
In mingled glory rise.

The murmur of their boughs and streams [2]
Speaks pride as well as bliss;
And that blue heaven expanding seems
The circling hills to kiss.

But, where is he to-day, to-day?
No—whisper not to me—
"I will not, dreamer, only say *
Where may thy lover be;

"Is he upon some distant shore
Or is he on the sea;
Or is the heart thou dost adore
A faithless heart to thee?"

The heart I love and you deride
Is changeless as the grave,
And neither foreign lands divide
Nor yet the ocean's wave.

"Then why should trouble cloud that brow
And tears those eyes bedim,
Reply this once—is it that thou
Hast faithless been to him?"

I dreamt, one dark and stormy night,
When winter winds were wild

The continuation of this poem may have been on a separate leaf which
has not been found.

[1] Cancelled in the manuscript.   [2] Cancelled in the manuscript.

D8

I gazed upon the cloudless moon,
And loved her all the night,
Till morning came and radiant noon
And I forgot her light—

No, not forgot—eternally
Remains its memory dear;
But could the day seem dark to me
Because the night was fair?

C11

III.   July 26, 1839

Shed no tears o'er that tomb
For there are Angels weeping;
Mourn not him whose doom
Heaven itself is mourning.
Look how in sable gloom
The clouds are earthward sweeping,
And earth receives them home,
Even darker clouds returning.

Is it when good men die
That sorrow wakes above?
Grieve saints when other spirits fly
To swell their choir of love?

Ah no, with louder sound
The golden harp-strings quiver
When good men gain the happy ground
Where they must dwell for ever.

But he who slumbers there,
His bark will strive no more
Across the waters of despair
To reach that glorious shore.

The time of grace is past
And mercy scorned and tried
Forsakes to utter wrath at last
The soul so steeled by pride.

That wrath will never spare,
Will never pity know,
Will mock its victim's maddened prayer,
Will triumph in his woe.

Shut from his Maker's smile
The accursed man shall be:
Compassion [1] reigns a little while,
Revenge [2] eternally.

C12

112.   A.A.A.

Sleep not, dream not; this bright day
Will not, cannot last for aye;
Bliss like thine is bought by years
Dark with torment and with tears.

Sweeter far than placid pleasure,
Purer, higher, beyond measure,
Yet alas the sooner turning
Into hopeless, endless mourning.

I love thee, boy; for all divine,
All full of God thy features shine.
Darling enthusiast, holy child,
Too good for this world's warring wild,
Too heavenly now but doomed to be
Hell-like in heart and misery.

[1] Alternative reading: For mercy.   [2] Alternative reading: But hate.

And what shall change that angel brow
And quench that spirit's glorious glow?
Relentless laws that disallow
True virtue and true joy below.

And blame me not, if, when the dread
Of suffering clouds thy youthful head,
If when by crime and sorrow tost
Thy wandering bark is wrecked and lost

I too depart, I too decline,
And make thy path no longer mine.
'Tis thus that human minds will turn,
All doomed alike to sin and mourn
Yet all with long gaze fixed afar,
Adoring virtue's distant star.

J284

113.   July 27, 1839

Mild the mist upon the hill,
Telling not of storms to-morrow;
No; the day has wept its fill,
Spent its store of silent sorrow.

Oh, I'm gone back to the days of youth,
I am a child once more;
And 'neath my father's sheltering roof,
And near the old hall door,

I watch this cloudy evening fall,
After a day of rain:
Blue mists, sweet mists of summer pall
The horizon's mountain-chain.

The damp stands in the long, green grass
As thick as morning's tears;

And dreamy scents of fragrance pass
That breathe of other years.

D14

114.   August 12, 1839

How long will you remain? The midnight hour
Has tolled the last note from the minster tower.*
Come, come: the fire is dead, the lamp burns low,
Your eyelids droop, a weight is on your brow.
Your cold hands hardly hold the useless pen; *
Come: morn will give recovered strength again.

"No: let me linger; leave me, let me be
A little longer in this reverie.
I'm happy now, and would you tear away
My blissful dream, that never comes with day; *
A vision dear, though false, for well my mind
Knows what a bitter waking waits behind?"

"Can there be pleasure in this shadowy room,
With windows yawning on intenser gloom,
And such a dreary wind so bleakly sweeping
Round walls where only you are vigil keeping?
Besides, your face has not a sign of joy,
And more than tearful sorrow fills your eye.
Look on those woods, look on that heaven lorn,*
And think how changed they'll be to-morrow morn:
The dome of heaven expanding bright and blue,
The leaves, the green grass, sprinkled thick with dew,*
And wet mists rising on the river's breast,*
And wild birds bursting from their songless nest,
And your own children's merry voices chasing
The fancies grief, not pleasure, has been tracing." *

"Aye, speak of these, but can you tell me why
Day breathes such beauty over earth and sky,

And waking sounds revive, restore again
The hearts that all night long have throbbed in pain?
Is it not that the sunshine and the wind
Lure from its self the mourner's woe-worn mind; *
And all the joyous music breathing by,
And all the splendour of that cloudless sky,
Re-give him shadowy gleams of infancy,
And draw his tired gaze from futurity?

A redundant line follows the sixth line in the manuscript:
  No leave me let me linger yet 'tis long

E18

115.   It is not pride, it is not shame,
       That makes her leave the gorgeous hall;
       And though neglect her heart might tame
       She mourns not for her sudden fall.

       'Tis true she stands among the crowd
       An unmarked and an unloved child,
       While each young comrade, blithe and proud,
       Glides through the maze of pleasure wild.

       And all do homage to their will,
       And all seem glad their voice to hear;
       She heeds not that, but hardly still
       Her eye can hold the quivering tear.

       What made her weep, what made her glide
       Out to the park this dreary day,
       And cast her jewelled chains aside,
       And seek a rough and lonely way,

       And down beneath a cedar's shade
       On the wet grass regardless lie,

With nothing but its gloomy head
Between her and the showery sky? *

I saw her stand in the gallery long,
Watching the little children there,
As they were playing the pillars among
And bounding down the marble stair.

The last verse has been printed as a separate fragment.
Hitherto, the poem has been dated August 13, 1839, but the manuscript, E18, a torn scrap of paper, bears no date.

A5

116.   August 30, 1839

Fair sinks the summer evening now
In softened glory round my home;
The sky upon its holy brow
Wears not a cloud that speaks of gloom.

The old tower, shrined in golden light,
Looks down on the descending sun—
So gently evening blends with night,
You scarce can say that day is done.

And this is just the joyous hour
When we were wont to burst away,
To 'scape from labour's tyrant power
And cheerfully go out to play.

Then why is all so sad and lone?
No merry foot-step on the stair—
No laugh—no heart-awaking tone,
But voiceless silence everywhere.

I've wandered round our garden-ground,
And still it seemed, at every turn,

That I should greet approaching feet,
And words upon the breezes borne.

In vain—they will not come to-day,
And morning's beam will rise as drear;
Then tell me—are they gone for aye
Our sun blinks through the mists of care?

Ah no; reproving Hope doth say,
Departed joys 'tis fond to mourn,
When every storm that hides their ray *
Prepares a more divine return.

D16

117.   September 6, 1839

Alcona, in its changing mood
My soul will sometimes overfly
The long, long years of solitude
That 'twixt our time of meeting lie.*

Hope and despair in turns arise
This doubting, dreading heart to move;
And now, 'mid smiles and bitter sighs,
Tell how I fear, tell how I love.

And now I say, "In Areon Hall—" *
(Alas that such a dream should come,
When well I know, whate'er befall,
That Areon is no more my ¹ home.)

Yet, let me say, "In Areon Hall *
The first faint red of morning shines,
And one right gladly to its call
The restless breath of grief resigns.

¹ Or "thy."

Her faded eye, her pallid face,
Would woo the soft, awaking wind;
All earth is breathing of the peace
She long has sought but cannot find.

How sweet it is to watch the mist
From that bright silent lake ascend,
And high o'er wood and mountain crest
With heaven's grey clouds as greyly blend.

How sweet it is to mark those clouds
Break brightly in the rising day;
To see the sober veil that shrouds
This summer morning melt away.

O sweet to some, but not to her;
Unm[ark]edst [1] once at Nature's shrine,*
She now kneels down a worshipper,
A mad adorer, love, to thine.

The time is come when hope, that long
Revived and sank, at length is o'er; *
When faith in him, however strong,
Dare prompt her to believe no more.

The tears which day by day o'erflowed
Their heart-deep source begin to freeze;
And, as she gazes on the road
That glances through those spreading [2] trees,

No throbbing flutter checks her breath
To mark a horseman hastening by;
Her haggard brow is calm as death,*
And cold like death her dreary eye."

[1] The letters within brackets are too indistinct to read in the manuscript and are, therefore, conjectural.
[2] Word cancelled in the manuscript and no word substituted.

The poem has not previously been included in an edition of Emily Jane Brontë's poems, but was printed in the *Brontë Society Publications* (1938), pp. 160–162.

C9

118. SONG October 15, 1839

O between distress and pleasure
Fond affection cannot be;
Wretched hearts in vain would treasure
Friendship's joys when others flee.

Well I know thine eye would never
Smile, while mine grieved, willingly; *
Yet I know thine eye for ever
Could not weep in sympathy.

Let us part, the time is over
When I thought and felt like thee;
I will be an Ocean rover,
I will sail the desert sea.

Isles there are beyond its billow:
Lands where woe may wander free;
And, beloved, thy midnight pillow
Will be soft unwatched by me.

Not on each returning morrow
When thy heart bounds ardently
Need'st thou then dissemble sorrow,
Marking my despondency.

Day by day some dreary token
Will forsake thy memory
Till at last all old links broken
I shall be a dream to thee.

E7

119.   October, 1839

There was a time when my cheek burned
To give such scornful fiends the lie; *
Ungoverned nature madly spurned
The law that bade it not defy.
O in the days of ardent youth
I would have given my life for truth.

For truth, for right, for liberty,
I would have gladly, freely died;
And now I calmly hear and see *
The vain man smile, the fool deride;
Though not because my heart is tame,
Though not for fear, though not for shame.

My soul still chafes at every tone *
Of selfish and self-blinded error; *
My breast still braves the world alone,
Steeled as it ever was to terror;
Only I know, however I frown,
The same world will go rolling on.

A14

120.   October 29, 1839

The wind, I hear it sighing
With Autumn's saddest sound;
Withered leaves as thick are lying
As spring-flowers on the ground.

This dark night has won me
To wander far away;

Old feelings gather fast upon me
Like vultures round their prey.

Kind were they once, and cherished,
But cold and cheerless now;
I would their lingering shades had perished
When their light left my brow.

'Tis like old age pretending
The softness of a child,
My altered, hardened spirit bending
To meet their fancies wild.

Yet could I with past pleasures
Past woe's oblivion buy,
That by the death of my dearest treasures
My deadliest pains might die,

O then another daybreak
Might haply dawn above,
Another summer gild my cheek,
My soul, another love.

A15

121.   LOVE AND FRIENDSHIP

Love is like the wild rose-briar,
Friendship like the holly-tree—
The holly is dark when the rose-briar blooms
But which will bloom most constantly?

The wild rose-briar is sweet in spring,
Its summer blossoms scent the air;
Yet wait till winter comes again
And who will call the wild-briar fair?

Then scorn the silly rose-wreath now
And deck thee with the holly's sheen,
That when December blights thy brow
He still may leave thy garland green.

H481

LOVE AND FRIENDSHIP

Love is like the wild rose-briar

The text as printed agrees with the manuscript.

In 1879, this poem was wrongly attributed to Charlotte Brontë, when it was set to music and published by W. Marriott and Sons, the title-page reading, "The Poetry by Charlotte Brontë, the Music by Einna."

A16

122. There should be no despair for you
While nightly stars are burning,
While evening sheds its silent dew *
Or sunshine gilds the morning.*

There should be no despair, though tears
May flow down like a river:
Are not the best beloved of years
Around your heart forever?

They weep—you weep—it must be so;
Winds sigh as you are sighing;
And Winter pours its grief in snow *
Where Autumn's leaves are lying.

Yet they revive, and from their fate *
Your fate cannot be parted,
Then journey onward, not elate,*
But *never* broken-hearted.*

G110

SYMPATHY

There should be no despair for you
Line 3 While evening pours its silent dew
     4 And sunshine gilds the morning
    11 And Winter sheds its grief in snow
    13 Yet these revive, and from their fate
    15 Then journey on, if not elate
    16 Still, *never* broken-hearted!

A17

123.   November 14, 1839

"Well, some may hate, and some may scorn,
And some may quite forget thy name,
But my sad heart must ever mourn
Thy ruined hopes, thy blighted fame."

'Twas thus I thought, an hour ago,
Even weeping o'er that wretch's woe.
One word turned back my gushing tears,
And lit my altered eye with sneers.

"Then bless the friendly dust," I said,
"That hides thy unlamented head.
Vain as thou wert, and weak as vain,
The slave of falsehood, pride and pain,
My heart has nought akin to thine—
Thy soul is powerless over mine."

But these were thoughts that vanished too—
Unwise, unholy, and untrue—
Do I despise the timid deer
Because his limbs are fleet with fear?

Or would I mock the wolf's death-howl
Because his form is gaunt and foul?
Or hear with joy the leveret's cry
Because it cannot bravely die?

No! Then above his memory
Let pity's heart as tender be:
Say, "Earth lie lightly on that breast,
And, kind Heaven, grant that spirit rest!"

G138

STANZAS TO ——

Well, some may hate, and some may scorn

The text agrees with the manuscript, but the lines are equally spaced throughout.

The date on the author's manuscript, as well as the year of publication (1846), makes it clear that this poem does not refer to Patrick Branwell Brontë, the degenerate brother of the Brontë sisters. He died on September 24, 1848.

E3

124.   November 23, 1839

The wind was rough which tore
That leaf from its parent tree;
The fate was cruel which bore
Its withering corpse to me.*

Here are a number of dates: October 1st, July 7th, January 13th, etc., followed by:

We wander on, we have no rest,*
It is a dreary way.

What shadow is it
That ever moves before my eyes? *
It has a brow of ghostly whiteness.

E17

125.   His land may burst the galling chain,
His people may be free again,
For them a thousand hopes remain,
But hope is dead for him.
Soft falls the moonlight on the sea
Whose wild waves play at liberty,
And Gondal's wind sings solemnly
Its native midnight hymn.*

Around his prison walls it sings,
His heart is stirred through all its strings,
Because that sound remembrance brings
Of scenes that once have been.
His soul has left the storm below,*
And reached a realm of sunless snow; *
The region of unchanging woe,*
Made voiceless by despair.

And Gerald's land may burst its chain,*
His subjects may be free again;
For them a thousand hopes remain,
But hope is dead for him.
Set is his sun of liberty;
Fixed is his earthly destiny;
A few years of captivity,
And then a captive's tomb.

J269

126.   Start not! upon the minster wall,
Sunshine is shed in holy calm;
And, lonely though my footsteps fall,
The saints shall shelter thee from harm.

Shrink not if it be summer noon;
This shadow should night's welcome be.
These stairs are steep, but landed soon
We'll rest us long and quietly.

What though our path be o'er the dead?
They slumber soundly in the tomb;
And why should mortals fear to tread
The pathway to their future home?

D13

127.   Nov. 28   1839

That wind, I used to hear it swelling
With joy divinely deep;
You might have seen my hot tears welling,
But rapture made me weep.

I used to love on winter nights
To lie and dream alone
Of all the rare [1] and real delights
My early years had known; *

And oh, above the rest of those *
That coming time should bear,
Like heaven's own glorious stars they rose
Still beaming bright and fair.

J297

128.   December 14, 1839

I've been wandering in the greenwoods,
And 'mid flowery, smiling plains;
I've been listening to the dark floods,
To the thrush's thrilling strains.

---

[1] Or "hopes."

I have gathered the pale primrose,
And the purple violet sweet;
I've been where the asphodel grows,
And where lives the red deer fleet.

I've been to the distant mountain,
To the silver singing rill,
By the crystal murmuring fountain,
And the shady, verdant hill.

I've been where the poplar is springing
From the fair enamelled ground,
Where the nightingale is singing
With a solemn, plaintive sound.

E16

129. That dreary lake, that midnight sky,*
That wan moon struggling through the cloud;
That sullen murmur, whispering by,
As if it dared not speak aloud,
Fall on my heart so sadly now
Wither my joy so lonely *

Touch them not, they bloom and smile,
But their roots are withering all the while.
Ah

Apparently trial lines for the beginning of a poem which was not completed.

E10

130. Dec. 19, 1839

Heaven's glory shone where he was laid
In life's decline.
I turned me from that young saint's bed
To gaze on thine.

It was a summer day that saw
His spirit's flight;
Thine parted in a time of awe,
A winter-night.*

E6

131. Upon her soothing breast
She lulled her little child;
A winter sunset in the west,
A dreary glory smiled.*

———

132. I gazed within thine earnest eyes,
And read the sorrow brooding there;
I saw thy young breast heave with sighs,*
And envied such despair.

Go to the grave in youth's first woe! *
That doom was written long ago.*

Manuscripts E10 and E6 appear to be separate parts of what was once a single leaf, with E10 as the upper part.

B17

133. F. De Samara.   E.   January 6, 1840
WRITTEN IN THE GAALDINE PRISON CAVES
TO A.G.A.

Thy sun is near meridian height,
And my sun sinks in endless night;
But, if that night bring only sleep,
Then I shall rest, while thou wilt weep.

And say not that my early tomb
Will give me to a darker doom:

Shall these long, agonising years
Be punished by eternal tears?

No; *that* I feel can never be; *
10 A God of *hate* could hardly bear
To watch through all eternity
His own creations dread despair!

The pangs that wring my mortal breast,
Must claim from Justice lasting rest;
Enough, that this departing breath
Will pass in anguish worse than death.

If I have sinned, long, long ago
That sin was purified by woe:
I've suffered on through night and day;
20 I've trod a dark and frightful way.

Earth's wilderness was round me spread;
Heaven's tempests beat my naked head;
I did not kneel: in vain would prayer
Have sought one gleam of mercy there!

How could I ask for pitying love,
When that grim concave frowned above,
Hoarding its lightnings to destroy
My only and my priceless joy?

They struck—and long may Eden shine
30 Ere I would call its glories mine:
All Heaven's undreamt felicity
Could never blot the past from me.

No; years may cloud and death may sever,
But what is done is done for ever;
And thou, false friend and treacherous guide,
Go, sate thy cruel heart with pride.

Go, load my memory with shame;
Speak but to curse my hated name;
My tortured limbs in dungeons bind,
40 And spare my life to kill my mind.

Leave me in chains and darkness now;
And when my very soul is worn,
When reason's light has left my brow,
And madness cannot feel thy scorn,

Then come again—thou wilt not shrink;
I know thy soul is free from fear—
The last full cup of triumph drink,
Before the blank of death be there.

Thy raving, dying victim see,
50 Lost, cursed, degraded, all for thee!
Gaze on the wretch, recall to mind
His golden days left long behind.

Does memory sleep in Lethean rest? *
Or wakes its whisper in thy breast?
O memory, wake! Let scenes return
That even her haughty heart must mourn! *

Reveal, where o'er a lone green wood
The moon of summer pours,
Far down from heaven, its silver flood,
60 On deep Elderno's shores.*

There, lingering in the wild embrace
Youth's warm affections gave,
She sits and fondly seems to trace
His features in the wave.

And while on that reflected face
Her eyes intently dwell,

"Fernando, sing to-night," she says,
The lays I love so well."

He smiles and sings, though every air
70 Betrays the faith of yesterday;
His soul is glad to cast for her
Virtue and faith and Heaven away.

Well thou hast paid me back my love!
But if there be a God above
Whose arm is strong, whose word is true,
This hell shall wring thy spirit too!

A18

134.   March, 1840

Far, far away is mirth withdrawn;
'Tis three long hours before the morn,
And I watch lonely, drearily:
So come, thou shade, commune with me.

Deserted one! thy corpse lies cold,
And mingled with a foreign mould.
Year after year the grass grows green
Above the dust where thou hast been.

I will not name thy blighted name,
Tarnished by unforgotten shame;
Though not because my bosom torn
Joins the mad world in all its scorn.

Thy phantom face is dark with woe;
Tears have left ghastly traces there:
Those ceaseless tears! I wish their flow
Could quench thy wild despair.

They deluge my heart like the rain
On cursed Gomorrah's howling plain;
Yet when I hear thy foes deride
I must cling closely to thy side.

Our mutual foes—they will not rest
From trampling on thy buried breast;
Glutting their hatred with the doom
They picture thine, beyond the tomb.

But God is not like human-kind;
Man cannot read the Almighty mind;
Vengeance will never torture thee,
Nor hunt thy soul eternally.

Then do not in this night of grief,
This time of overwhelming fear,
O do not think that God can leave,
Forget, forsake, refuse to hear!

What have I dreamt? He lies asleep *
With whom my heart would vainly weep:
He rests, and *I* endure the woe
That left his spirit long ago.

A13

135.   April, 1840

It is too late to call thee now:
I will not nurse that dream again;
For every joy that lit my brow
Would bring its after-storm of pain.

Besides, the mist is half withdrawn;
The barren mountain-side lies bare;
And sunshine and awaking morn
Paint no more golden visions there.

Yet, ever in my grateful breast,
Thy darling shade shall cherished be;
For God alone doth know how blest
My early years have been in thee!

A10

136.   May 4, 1840

I'll not weep that thou art going to leave me,
There's nothing lovely here;
And doubly will the dark world grieve me
While thy heart suffers there.

I'll not weep, because the summer's glory
Must always end in gloom;
And, follow out the happiest story—
It closes with the tomb! *

And I am weary of the anguish
Increasing winters bear;
I'm sick to see the spirit languish *
Through years of dead despair.

So, if a tear, when thou art dying,
Should haply fall from me,
It is but that my soul is sighing
To go and rest with thee.

G148

STANZAS

I'll not weep that thou art going to leave me
Line 8 It closes with a tomb!
      11 Weary to watch the spirit languish

B3

137. A.G.A. to A.S.[1]　　　　　E.　　$\begin{cases} \text{May 6, 1840} \\ \text{July 28, 1843} \end{cases}$

At such a time, in such a spot,
The world seems made of light;
Our blissful hearts remember not
How surely follows night.

I cannot, Alfred, dream of aught
That casts a shade of woe;
That heaven is reigning in my thought,
Which wood and wave and earth have caught
From skies that overflow.

That heaven which my sweet lover's brow
Has won me to adore,
Which from his blue eyes beaming now
Reflects a still intenser glow
Than nature's heaven can pour.

I know our souls are all divine;
I know that when we die,
What seems the vilest, even like thine
A part of God himself shall shine
In perfect purity.

But coldly breaks November's day;
Its changes, charmless all;
Unmarked, unloved, they pass away;
We do not wish one hour to stay,
Nor sigh at evening's fall.

[1] Lord Alfred of Aspin Castle.

And glorious is the gladsome rise
Of June's rejoicing morn;
And who with unregretful eyes
Can watch the lustre leave its skies
To twilight's shade forlorn?

Then art thou not my golden June
All mist and tempest free?
As shines earth's sun in summer noon
So heaven's sun shines in thee.

Let others seek its beams divine
In cell and cloister drear;
But I have found a fairer shrine
And happier worship here.

By dismal rites they win their bliss—
By penance, fasts, and fears;
I have one rite: a gentle kiss;
One penance: tender tears.

O could it thus forever be
That I might so adore;
I'd ask for all eternity
To make a paradise for me,
My love—and nothing more!

The title "Love's Contentment" which has been printed with this
poem is from a transcript by the Reverend A. B. Nicholls.

A11

138.   May 18, 1840

If grief for grief can touch thee,
If answering woe for woe,

If any ruth can melt thee,
Come to me now!

I cannot be more lonely,
More drear I cannot be!
My worn heart throbs so wildly
'Twill break for thee.

And when the world despises,
When heaven repels my prayer,
Will not mine angel comfort?
Mine idol hear?

Yes, by the tears I've poured [thee],
By all my hours of pain,
O I shall surely win thee,
Beloved, again!

E11

139.   May 19, 1840

'Tis moonlight, summer moonlight,
All soft, and still, and fair;
The solemn hour of midnight *
Breathes sweetly everywhere.*

But most where trees are sending
Their breezy boughs on high,
Or stooping low are lending
A shelter from the sky.

And there in those wild bowers
A lovely form is laid;
Green grass and dew-steeped flowers
Wave gently round her head.

A7

140.　　　　　　THE NIGHT-WIND　　September 11, 1840

In summer's mellow midnight,
A cloudless moon shone through
Our open parlour window
And rosetrees wet with dew.

I sat in silent musing,
The soft wind waved my hair:
It told me Heaven was glorious.
And sleeping Earth was fair.

I needed not its breathing
To bring such thoughts to me,
But still it whispered lowly,
"How dark the woods will be!

"The thick leaves in my murmur
Are rustling like a dream,
And all their myriad voices
Instinct with spirit seem."

I said, "Go, gentle singer,
Thy wooing voice is kind,
But do not think its music
Has power to reach my mind.

"Play with the scented flower,
The young tree's supple bough,
And leave my human feelings
In their own course to flow."

The wanderer would not leave [1] me;
Its kiss grew warmer still—

[1] Or "heed."

"O come," it sighed so sweetly,
"I'll win thee 'gainst thy will.

"Have we not been from childhood friends?
Have I not loved thee long?
As long as thou hast loved the night
Whose silence wakes my song.

"And when thy heart is laid at rest
Beneath the church-yard stone
I shall have time enough to mourn
And thou to be alone."

This poem was first printed in 1850, between poems numbered 147 and 148 in the present collection, with a few introductory words by Charlotte Brontë to each of the three poems.

H479

Here again is the same mind in converse with a like abstraction. "The Night-Wind," breathing through an open window, has visited an ear which discerned language in its whispers. (*Note by Charlotte Brontë*)

THE NIGHT-WIND

> *In summer's mellow midnight*
Line 25 The wanderer would not heed me
    29 "Were we not friends from childhood?
    31 As long as thou, the solemn night
    33 "And when thy heart is resting
       Beneath the church-aisle stone,
     I shall have time for mourning,
     And *thou* for being alone."

Charlotte Brontë altered "church-yard" in the last verse of the manuscript to "church-aisle." Emily Jane Brontë was not buried in the churchyard, but beneath the aisle in Haworth Church.

D15

141.   September 17, 1840

E.J.B.
R. Gleneden (?)

Companions, all day long we've stood,
The wild winds restless blowing;
All day we've watched the darkened flood
Around our vessel flowing.

Sunshine has never smiled since morn,
And clouds have gathered drear,
And heavier hearts would feel forlorn
And weaker minds would fear.

But look in each young shipmate's eyes
10 Lit by the evening flame,
And see how little stormy skies
Our joyous blood can tame.

No glance the same expression wears,
No lip the same soft smile;
Yet kindness warms and courage cheers:
Nerves every breast the while.

It is the hour of dreaming now,
The red fire brightly gleams;
And sweetest in a red fire's glow *
20 The hour of dreaming seems.

I may not trace the thoughts of all,
But some I read as well
As I can hear the ocean's fall
And sullen surging swell.

Edmund's swift soul is gone before:
It threads a forest wide,
Whose towers are bending to the shore *
And gazing on the tide.

And one is there; I know the voice,
30 The thrilling, stirring tone
That makes his bounding pulse rejoice,
Yet makes not *his* alone.

Mine own hand longs to clasp her hand,
Mine eye to greet her eye;
Win, white sails, win Zedora's strand *
And Ula's Eden sky.*

Mary and Flora, oft their gaze
Is clouded pensively,
And what that earnest aspect says
40 Is all revealed to me.

'Tis but two years, or little more,
Since first they dared that main;
And such a night may well restore
That first time back again.

The smothered sigh, the lingering late,
The longed-for, dreaded hour,
The parting at the moss-grown gate,
The last look on the tower:

I know they think of these, and then
50 The evening's gathering gloom,
And they alone, with foreign men
To guard their cabin room.

The last four verses are now printed for the first time in an edition of
Emily Jane Brontë's poems; but the whole poem was printed in the
Brontë Society Publications (1938), pp. 169–170.

E4

142. There let thy bleeding branch atone
For every torturing tear:
Shall my young sins, my sins alone,
Be everlasting here?

Who bade thee keep that cursed name *
A pledge for memory?
As if Oblivion ever came
To breathe its bliss on me;

As if, through all the 'wildering maze
Of mad hours left behind,
I once forgot the early days
That thou wouldst call to mind.

B21

143. E.J.   THE DEATH OF A.G.A.   {January, 1841
                                      {May, 1844

Were they shepherds, who sat all day
On that brown mountain-side? *
But neither staff nor dog had they,
Nor woolly flock to guide.

They were clothed in savage attire;
Their locks were dark and long;
And at each belt a weapon dire,
Like bandit-knife, was hung.

One was a woman, tall and fair;
10 A princess she might be,
From her stately form, and her features rare,
And her look of majesty.

But, oh, she had a sullen frown,
A lip of cruel scorn,
As sweet tears never melted down
Her cheeks since she was born!

'Twas well she had no sceptre to wield,
No subject land to sway:
Fear might have made her vassals yield,
20 But Love had been far away.

Yet, Love was even at her feet *
In his most burning mood:
That Love which will the Wicked greet
As kindly as the Good—

And he was noble too, who bowed *
So humbly by her side,
Entreating, till his eyes o'erflowed,
Her spirit's icy pride.

"Angelica, from my very birth
30 I have been nursed in strife:
And lived upon this weary Earth
A wanderer, all my life.

"The baited tiger could not be
So much athirst for gore:
For men and laws have tortured me
Till I can bear no more.

"The guiltless blood upon my hands
Will shut me out from Heaven;
And here, and even in foreign lands,
40 I cannot find a haven.

"And in all space, and in all time,*
And through Eternity,

To aid a Spirit lost in crime,
I have no hope but thee.

"Yet will I swear, No saint on high *
A truer faith could prove;
No angel, from that holy sky,
Could give thee purer love.

"For thee, through never-ending years,
50 I'd suffer endless pain;
But—only give me back my tears;
Return my love again!"

Many a time, unheeded, thus
The reckless man would pray;
But something woke an answering flush
On his lady's brow to-day;
And her eye flashed flame, as she turned to speak,
In concord with her reddening cheek:

"I've known a hundred kinds of love:
60 *All* made the loved one rue;
And what is thine that it should prove,
Than other love, more true?

"Listen; I've known a burning heart
To which my own was given;
Nay, not in passion; do not start—*
Our love was love from heaven;
At least, if heavenly love be born
In the pure light of childhood's morn—
Long ere the poison-tainted air
70 From this world's plague-fen rises there.

"That heart was like a tropic sun *
That kindles all it shines upon;
And never Magian devotee *

Gave worship half so warm as I;
And never radiant [1] bow could be
So welcome in a stormy sky.
My soul dwelt with her day and night:
She was my all-sufficing light,
My childhood's mate, my girlhood's guide,
80 My only blessing, only pride.

"But cursed be the very earth
That gave that fiend her fatal birth! *
With her own hand she bent the bow
That laid my best affections low,
Then mocked my grief and scorned my prayers
And drowned my bloom of youth in tears.
Warnings, reproaches, both were vain—
What recked she of another's pain?
My dearer self she would not spare—
90 From Honour's voice she turned his ear:
First made her love his only stay,
Then snatched the treacherous prop away.
Douglas, he pleaded bitterly;
He pleaded as *you* plead to me
For lifelong chains or timeless tomb
Or any but an Exile's doom.
We both were scorned—both sternly driven
To shelter 'neath a foreign heaven;
And darkens o'er that dreary time
100 A wildering dream of frenzied crime.
I will not now those days recall;
The oath within that caverned hall
And its fulfilment, those you know—*
We both together struck the blow.
But—you can never know the pain
That my lost heart did then sustain,
When severed wide by guiltless gore
I felt that *one* could love no more! *

[1] Or "glittering."

Back, maddening thought!—The grave is deep
110 Where my Amedeus lies asleep,
And I have long forgot to weep.

"Now hear me: in these regions wild
I saw to-day my enemy.
Unarmed, as helpless as a child
She slumbered on a sunny lea.
Two friends—no other guard had she,
And they were wandering on the braes
And chasing in regardless glee
The wild goat o'er his dangerous ways.
120 My hand was raised—my knife was bare;
With stealthy tread I stole along;
But a wild bird sprang from his hidden lair
And woke her with a sudden song.
Yet moved she not: she only raised
Her lids and on the bright sun gazed,
And uttered such a dreary sigh
I thought just then she should not die
Since living was such misery.
Now, Douglas, for our hunted band—
130 For future joy and former woe—
Assist me with thy heart and hand
To send to hell my mortal foe.
Her friends fell first, that she may drain *
A deeper cup of bitterer pain.
Yonder they stand and watch the waves
Dash in among the echoing caves—
Their farewell sight of earth and sea!
Come, Douglas, rise and go with me."

. . . .

The lark sang clearly overhead,
140 And sweetly hummed the bee;
And softly, round their dying bed,
The wind blew from the sea.

Fair Surry would have raised her eyes
To see that water shine;
To see once more in mountain skies
The summer sun decline:

But ever, on her fading cheek,
The languid lid would close,
As weary that such light should break *
150 Its much-desired repose.

And she was waning fast away—
Even Memory's voice grew dim;
Her former life's eventful day
Had dwindled to a dream;

And hardly could her mind recall
One thought of joy or pain;
That cloud was gathering over all
Which never clears again.

In vain, in vain; you need not gaze
160 Upon those features now!
That sinking head you need not raise,
Nor kiss that pulseless brow.

Let out the grief that chokes your breath; *
Lord Lesley, set it free:
The sternest eye, for such a death,
Might fill with sympathy.

The tresses o'er her bosom spread
Were by a faint breeze blown:
"Her heart is beating," Lesley said;
170 "She is not really gone!"

And still that form he fondly pressed;
And still of hope he dreamed;

Nor marked how from his own young breast
Life's crimson current streamed.

At last, the sunshine left the ground;
The laden bee flew home;
The deep down sea, with sadder sound,*
Impelled its waves to foam;

And the corpse grew heavy on his arm,*
180 The starry heaven grew dim,
The summer night, so mild and warm,
Felt wintery chill to him.

A troubled shadow o'er his eye
Came down, and rested there;
The moors and sky went swimming by,
Confused and strange and drear.

He faintly prayed, "Oh, Death, delay
Thy last fell dart to throw,
Till I can hear my Sovereign say,
190 'The traitors' heads are low!'

"God, guard her life, since not to me
That dearest boon was given;
God, bless her arm with victory *
Or bless not me with heaven!"

Then came the cry of agony,
The pang of parting pain;
And he had overpassed the sea
That none can pass again.

. . . .

Douglas leaned above the well,
200 Heather banks around him rose;
Bright and warm the sunshine fell
On that spot of sweet repose,

With the blue heaven bending o'er,
And the soft wind singing by,
And the clear stream evermore
Mingling harmony.

On the shady side reclined,
He watched its waters play,
And sound and sight had well combined
210 To banish gloom away.

A voice spoke near: "She'll come," it said,
"And, Douglas, thou shalt be
My love, although the very dead
Should rise to rival thee!

"Now, only let thine arm be true
And nerved, like mine, to kill;
And Gondal's royal race shall rue
This day on Elmor Hill!"

They wait not long; the rustling heath
220 Betrays their royal foe;
With hurried step and panting breath
And cheek almost as white as death,
Augusta sprang below—

Yet marked she not where Douglas lay;
She only saw the well—
The tiny fountain, churning spray
Within its mossy cell.

"Oh, I have wrongs to pay," she cried,*
"Give life, give vigour now!"
230 And, stooping by the water's side,
She drank its crystal flow.*

And brightly, with that draught, came back
The glory of her matchless eye,

As, glancing o'er the moorland track,
She shook her head impatiently.

Nor shape, nor shade—the mountain flocks
Quietly feed in grassy dells;
Nor sound, except the distant rocks
Echoing to their bells.

240 She turns—she meets the Murderer's gaze;
Her own is scorched with a sudden blaze—
The blood streams down her brow;
The blood streams through her coal-black hair—
She strikes it off with little care;
She scarcely feels it flow; *
For she has marked and known him too
And his own heart's ensanguined dew
Must slake her vengeance now!

False friend! no tongue save thine can tell
250 The mortal strife that then befell;
But, ere night darkened down,
The stream in silence sang once more;
And, on its green bank, bathed in gore,
Augusta lay alone!

False Love! no earthly eye did see,
Yet Heaven's pure eye regarded thee,
Where thy own Douglas bled—
How thou didst turn in mockery
From his last hopeless agony,
260 And leave the hungry hawk to be
Sole watcher of the dead!

.   .   .   .

Was it a deadly swoon?
Or was her spirit really gone?
And the cold corpse, beneath the moon,*
Laid like another mass of dust and stone?

The moon was full that night,
The sky was almost like the day:
You might have seen the pulse's play
Upon her forehead white;

270 You might have seen the dear, dear sign of life *
In her uncovered eye,
And her cheek changing in the mortal strife
Betwixt the pain to live and agony to die.

But nothing mutable was there;
The face, all deadly fair,
Showed a fixed impress of keen suffering past,
And the raised lid did show
No wandering gleam below
But a stark anguish, self-destroyed at last.*

280 Long he gazed and held his breath,
Kneeling on the blood-stained heath;
Long he gazed those lids beneath
Looking into Death!

Not a word from his followers fell:
They stood by, mute and pale;
That black treason uttered well
Its own heart-harrowing tale.

But earth was bathed in other gore:
There were crimson drops across the moor;
290 And Lord Eldred, glancing round,
Saw those tokens on the ground:

"Bring him back!" he hoarsely said;
"Wounded is the traitor fled;
Vengeance may hold but minutes brief,
And you have all your lives for grief."

He is left alone—he sees the stars
Their quiet course continuing,
And, far away, down Elmor scars
He hears the stream its waters fling.

300 That lulling monotone did sing
Of broken rock and shaggy glen,
Of welcome for the moorcock's wing;
But, not of wail for men!

Nothing in heaven or earth to show *
One sign of sympathizing woe—
And nothing but that agony,
In her now unconscious eye,
To weigh upon the labouring breast
And prove she did not pass at rest.

310 But he who watched, in thought had gone,
Retracing back her lifetime flown:
Like sudden ghosts, to memory came
Full many a face and many a name,
Full many a heart, that, in the tomb,
He almost deemed might have throbbed again,
Had they but known her dreary doom,
Had they but seen their idol there,
A wreck of desolate despair,
Left to the wild birds of the air
320 And mountain winds and rain.
For him—no tear his stern eye shed
As he looked down upon the dead.

"Wild morn," he thought, "and doubtful noon;
But yet it was a glorious sun,
Though comet-like its course was run.
That sun should never have been given
To burn and dazzle in the heaven,
Or night has quenched it far too soon!

And thou art gone—with all thy pride;
330 Thou, so adored, so deified!
Cold as the earth, unweeting now
Of love, or joy, or mortal woe.
For what thou wert I would not grieve,
But much for what thou wert to be—
That life so stormy and so brief,
That death has wronged us more than thee.
Thy passionate youth was nearly past,
The opening sea seemed smooth at last;
Yet vainly flowed the calmer wave
340 Since fate had not decreed to save.
And vain too must the sorrow be
Of those who live to mourn for thee;
But Gondal's foes shall not complain
That thy dear blood was poured in vain!"

E9

144.   Feb. 27, 1841

And like myself lone, wholly lone,
It sees the day's long sunshine glow;
And like myself it makes its moan
In unexhausted woe.

Give we the hills our equal prayer:
Earth's breezy hills and heaven's blue sea;
We ask for nothing further here *
But our own hearts and liberty.*

Ah! could my hand unlock its chain,
How gladly would I watch it soar,*
And ne'er regret and ne'er complain
To see its shining eyes no more.

But let me think that if to-day
It pines in cold captivity,
To-morrow both shall soar away,
Eternally, entirely Free.

This poem and No. 145 have hitherto been printed as one poem, but there does not appear to be any connection between them. They are in separate and distinct manuscripts.

The title of "The Caged Bird" was added to this poem by Mr A. C. Benson in *Brontë Poems* (1915).

Below the poem in the manuscript is written, apparently by Mr T. J. Wise, the name "Anne," but the poem is in the handwriting of Emily Jane Brontë.

E15

145.   M.A.A.

Methinks this heart should rest awhile,
So stilly round the evening falls;
The veiled sun sheds no parting smile,*
Nor mirth, nor music wakes my halls.

I have sat lonely all the day
Watching the drizzly mist descend
And first conceal the hills in grey
And then along the valleys wend.

And I have sat and watched the trees
And the sad flowers—how drear they blow:
Those flowers were formed to feel the breeze
Wave their light leaves in summer's glow.*

Yet their lives passed in gloomy woe
And hopeless comes its dark decline,
And I lament, because I know
That cold departure pictures mine.

                  *   *   *   *   *   *

A8

146. March 1, 1841

Riches I hold in light esteem
And Love I laugh to scorn
And lust of Fame was but a dream
That vanished with the morn—

And if I pray, the only prayer
That moves my lips for me
Is—"Leave the heart that now I bear
And give me liberty."

Yes, as my swift days near their goal
'Tis all that I implore—
Through life and death, a chainless soul *
With courage to endure!

G163

THE OLD STOIC

Riches I hold in light esteem
Line 11 In life and death a chainless soul

A6

147. May 16, 1841

Shall Earth no more inspire thee,
Thou lonely dreamer now?
Since passion may not fire thee
Shall Nature cease to bow?

Thy mind is ever moving
In regions dark to thee;

Recall its useless roving—
Come back and dwell with me.

I know my mountain breezes
Enchant and soothe thee still—
I know my sunshine pleases
Despite thy wayward will.

When day with evening blending
Sinks from the summer sky,
I've seen thy spirit bending
In fond idolatry.

I've watched thee every hour;
I know my mighty sway,
I know my magic power
To drive thy griefs away.

Few hearts to mortals given
On earth so wildly pine;
Yet none would ask a Heaven
More like this Earth than thine.

Then let my winds caress thee;
Thy comrade let me be—
Since nought beside can bless thee,
Return and dwell with me.

H478

The following little piece has no title, but in it the Genius of a solitary region seems to address his wandering and wayward votary, and to recall within his influence the proud mind which rebelled at times against what it most loved. (*Note by Charlotte Brontë*)

Shall earth no more inspire thee

Agrees with Manuscript A6.

A9

148. July 6, 1841

Aye, there it is! It wakes to-night
Sweet thoughts that will not die
And feeling's fires flash all as bright
As in the years gone by!

And I can tell by thine altered cheek
And by thy kindled gaze
And by the words thou scarce dost speak,
How wildly fancy plays.

Yes, I could swear that glorious wind
Has swept the world aside,
Has dashed its memory from thy mind
Like foam-bells from the tide—

And thou art now a spirit pouring
Thy presence into all—
The essence of the Tempest's roaring
And of the Tempest's fall—

A universal influence
From Thine own influence free;
A principle of life, intense,
Lost to mortality.

Thus truly when that breast is cold
Thy prisoned soul shall rise,
The dungeon mingle with the mould—
The captive with the skies.

H480

In these stanzas a louder gale has roused the sleeper on her pillow: the
wakened soul struggles to blend with the storm by which it is swayed.
(*Note by Charlotte Brontë*)

Ay—there it is! it wakes to-night
Line 2 Deep feelings I thought dead
3 Strong in the blast—quick gathering light—
4 The heart's flame kindles red
5 "Now I can tell by thine altered cheek
6 And by thine eyes' full gaze
15 The thunder of the tempest's roaring
16 The whisper of its fall
17 An universal influence

At the end of the poem Charlotte Brontë added 5 lines:

Nature's deep being, thine shall hold,
Her spirit all thy spirit fold,
    Her breath absorb thy sighs.
Mortal! though soon life's tale is told,
    Who once lives, never dies!

A19

149.   July 17, 1841

I see around me tombstones grey
Stretching their shadows far away.
Beneath the turf my footsteps tread
Lie low and lone the silent dead;
Beneath the turf, beneath the mould—
Forever dark, forever cold,
And my eyes cannot hold the tears
That memory hoards from vanished years;
For Time and Death and Mortal pain
Give wounds that will not heal again.
Let me remember half the woe
I've seen and heard and felt below,
And Heaven itself, so pure and blest,
Could never give my spirit rest.
Sweet land of light! thy children fair
Know nought akin to our despair;
Nor have they felt, nor can they tell

What tenants haunt each mortal cell,
What gloomy guests we hold within—
Torments and madness, tears and sin!
Well, may they live in extasy
Their long eternity of joy;
At least we would not bring them down
With us to weep, with us to groan.
No—Earth would wish no other sphere
To taste her cup of sufferings drear;
She turns from Heaven a careless eye
And only mourns that *we* must die!
Ah mother, what shall comfort thee
In all this boundless misery?
To cheer our eager eyes a while
We see thee smile; how fondly smile!
But who reads not through that tender glow
Thy deep, unutterable woe?
Indeed, no dazzling land above
Can cheat thee of thy children's love.
We all, in life's departing shine,
Our last dear longings blend with thine;
And struggle still and strive to trace
With clouded gaze, thy darling face.
We would not leave our native home
For *any* world beyond the Tomb.
No—rather on thy kindly breast
Let us be laid in lasting rest;
Or waken but to share with thee
A mutual immortality.

In the birthday diary fragment, written by Emily Jane Brontë on July 30, 1841, there is a slight reference to the Gondals (a fictitious northern race about whom she and her sister Anne had been writing prose stories and poems for some years): "The Gondolians are at present in a threatening state, but there is no open rupture as yet. All the princes and princesses of the Royalty are at the Palace of Instruction. I have a good many books on hand, but, I am sorry to say, as usual I make small progress with any."

On the same day, Anne Brontë wrote: "I wonder whether the Gondolians will still be flourishing [on July 30, 1845; see pages 233–234] and what will be their condition. I am now engaged in writing the fourth volume of Solala Vernon's life."

B15

150.   GERALDINE   E.   August 17, 1841

'Twas night; her comrades gathered all
Within their city's rocky wall;
When flowers were closed and day was o'er,
Their joyous hearts awoke the more.

But, lonely in her distant cave,
She heard the river's restless wave
Chafing its banks with dreamy flow:
Music for mirth and wail for woe.

Palm-trees and cedars towering high
10 Deepened the gloom of evening's sky;
And thick did raven ringlets veil
Her forehead, drooped like lily pale.

Yet I could hear my lady sing:
I knew she did not mourn;
For never yet from sorrow's spring
Such witching notes were born.

Thus poured she in that cavern wild
The voice of feelings warm,
As, bending o'er her beauteous child,
20 She clasped its sleeping form—

"Why sank so soon the summer sun
From our Zedora's skies? *
I was not tired, my darling one,
Of gazing in thine eyes.

"Methought the heaven, whence thou hast come,
Was lingering there awhile;
And Earth seemed such an alien home
They did not dare to smile.

"Methought each moment something strange
30 Within their circles shone,
And yet, through every magic change,
They were Brenzaida's own.*

"Methought—what thought I not, sweet love?
My whole heart centred there:
I breathed not but to send above
One gush of ardent prayer—

" 'Bless it, my gracious God,' I cried;
'Preserve thy mortal shrine;
For thine own sake, be thou its guide,
40 And keep it still divine!

" 'Say, sin shall never blanch that cheek,
Nor suffering charge that brow; *
Speak, in thy mercy, Maker, speak,
And seal it safe from woe!'

"Why did I doubt? In God's control
Our mutual fates remain;
And pure as now my angel's soul
Must go to Heaven again." *

The revellers in the city slept;
50 My lady, in her woodland bed;
I, watching o'er her slumber, wept *
As one who mourns the dead!

The last stanza appears to have been added to the manuscript after the succeeding poem, dated August 30, 1838, No. 76, had been written therein.

B12

151.   ROSINA   September 1, 1841

Weeks of wild delirium past,
Weeks of fevered pain;
Rest from suffering comes at last;
Reason dawns again.

It was a pleasant April day
Declining to the afternoon;
Sunshine upon her pillow lay
As warm as middle June.

It told her how unconsciously *
10 Early spring had hurried by;
Ah! Time has not delayed for me,"
She murmured with a sigh.

"Angora's hills have heard their tread;
The crimson flag is planted there;
Elderno's waves are rolling red,*
While *I* lie fettered here.

"Nay; rather, Gondal's shaken throne
Is now secure and free;
And my King Julius reigns alone,
20 Debtless, alas! to me."

Loud was the sudden gush of woe
From those who watched around;
Rosina turned, and sought to know
Why burst that boding sound.

"What then, my dreams are false?" she said;
"Come, maidens, answer me:

Has Almedore in battle bled? [1]
Have slaves subdued the free?

"I know it all: he could not bear
30 To leave me dying far away;
He fondly, madly lingered here
And we have lost the day!

"But check those coward sobs, and bring
My robes, and smoothe my tangled hair:
A noble victory you shall sing
For every hour's despair!

"When will he come? 'Twill soon be night:
He'll come when evening falls;
Oh, I shall weary for the light,
40 To leave my lonely halls!"

She turned her pallid face aside,
As she would seek repose;
But dark Ambition's thwarted pride
Forbade her lids to close.

And still on all who waited by
Oppressive mystery hung;
And swollen with grief was every eye,
And chained was every tongue.

They whispered nought but, "Lady, sleep;
50 Dear Lady, slumber now!
Had we not bitter cause to weep
While you were laid so low?

"And Hope can hardly deck the cheek
With sudden signs of cheer,
When it has worn through many a week
The stamp of anguish drear." *

[1] Or "fled."

Fierce grew Rosina's gloomy gaze;
She cried, "Dissemblers, own,*
Exina's arms in victory blaze; *
60 Brenzaida's crest is down?"

"Well, since it must be told, Lady,
Brenzaida's crest *is* down;
Brenzaida's sun is set, Lady,
His empire overthrown!

"He died beneath this [1] palace dome—*
True hearts on every side;
Among his guards, within his home
Our glorious Monarch died.

"I saw him fall, I saw the gore
70 From his heart's fountain swell,
And mingling on the marble floor
His murderer's life-blood fell.

And now, 'mid northern mountains lone,
His desert grave is made;
And, Lady, of your love alone
Remains a mortal shade!"

B28

152. A.S. TO G.S. . . .   December 19, 1841

I do not weep, I would not weep;
Our Mother needs no tears;
Dry thine eyes too, 'tis vain to keep
This causeless grief for years.

What though her brow be changed and cold,
Her sweet eyes closed for ever?
What though the stone—the darksome mould
Our mortal bodies sever?

[1] As in manuscript. Perhaps "his" was intended.

What though her hand smoothe ne'er again
Those silken locks of thine—
Nor through long hours of future pain
Her kind face o'er thee shine?

Remember still she is not dead,
She sees us, Gerald, now,*
Laid where her angel spirit fled
'Mid heath and frozen snow.

And from that world of heavenly light
Will she not always bend,
To guide us in our lifetime's night
And guard us to the end?

Thou know'st she will, and well may'st mourn *
That we are left below,
But not that she can ne'er return
To share our earthly woe.

The title which Charlotte Brontë gave to this poem when it was printed in 1850 is pencilled in her handwriting under the heading in the manuscript.

H488

ENCOURAGEMENT

I do not weep; I would not weep
Line 14 She sees us, sister, now
  21 Thou knowest she will; and thou may'st mourn

B37

153.   H.A. AND A.S.   May 17, 1842

In the same place, when Nature wore
The same celestial glow,

I'm sure I've seen those forms before *
But many springs ago;

And only *he* had locks of light,*
And *she* had raven hair; *
While now, his curls are dark as night,
And hers as morning fair.

Besides, I've dreamt of tears whose traces
Will never more depart,
Of agony that fast effaces
The verdure of the heart.

I dreamt one sunny day like this,
In this peerless month of May,
I saw her give the unanswered kiss
As his spirit passed away:

Those young eyes that so sweetly shine
Then looked their last adieu,
And pale Death changed that cheek divine
To his unchanging hue;

And earth was cast above the breast
That beats so warm and free *
Where her soft ringlets lightly rest *
And move responsively.*

Then she, upon the covered grave—
The grass grown grave, did lie:
A tomb not girt by Gondal's wave *
Nor arched by Gondal's sky.*

The sod was sparkling bright with dew,
But brighter still with tears,
That welled from mortal grief, I knew,
Which never heals with years.

And if he came not for her woe,
He would not now return;
He would not leave his sleep below
When she had ceased to mourn.

O Innocence, that cannot live
With heart-wrung anguish long—
Dear childhood's Innocence, forgive,
For I have done thee wrong!

The bright rose-buds, those hawthorns shroud
Within their perfumed bower,
Have never closed beneath a cloud,
Nor bent before a shower—*

Had darkness once obscured their sun
Or kind dew turned to rain,
No storm-cleared sky that ever shone
Could win such bliss again.

From the date in the author's manuscript, this poem appears to have
been written when she and her sister, Charlotte, were pupils at the
Heger Pensionnat in Brussels (from February 8 to November 6, 1842).

Beside the second verse in the manuscript is written in Charlotte
Brontë's hand: "who now has raven hair / and those eyes rival dark of
night / were all as morning fair"; and beside the ninth verse: "Whose
then the arms and whose the eyes / That clasp and watch her now"—
probably when she was selecting and altering poems for printing in 1850.

B8

154. WRITTEN IN ASPIN CASTLE E. $\begin{cases} \text{August 20, 1842} \\ \text{February 6, 1843} \end{cases}$

How do I love on summer nights
To sit within this Norman door,
Whose sombre portal hides the lights
Thickening above me evermore!

How do I love to hear the flow
Of Aspin's water murmuring low;
And hours long listen to the breeze
That sighs in Rockden's waving trees.*

To-night, there is no wind to wake
10 One ripple on the lonely lake; *
To-night, the clouds subdued and grey
Starlight and moonlight shut away.

'Tis calm and still and almost drear,
So utter is the solitude;
But still I love to linger here
And form my mood to nature's mood.

There's a wild walk beneath the rocks
Following the bend of Aspin's side;
'Tis worn by feet of mountain-flocks
20 That wander down to drink the tide.

Never by cliff and gnarlèd tree
Wound fairy path so sweet to me;
Yet of the native shepherds none,
In open day and cheerful sun,
Will tread its labyrinths alone;
Far less when evening's pensive hour
Hushes the bird and shuts the flower,
And gives to Fancy magic power
O'er each familiar tone.*

30 For round their hearths they'll tell the tale,
And every listener swears it true,
How wanders there a phantom pale
With spirit-eyes of dreamy blue.

It always walks with head declined,
Its long curls move not in the wind,*

Written in Aspin Castle —   L. August 20th 1842
                                   February 6th 1843

O Aspin

How do I love on summer nights
To sit within this Norman door
Whose sombre portal hides the light
Thickening above me evermore!

How do I love to hear the flow
Of Aspin, water murmuring low
And hours long listen to the breeze
That sighs in Rockden's waving trees

Tonight, there is no wind to wake
One ripple on the lonely lake
Tonight the clouds subdued and grey
Starlight and moonlight shut away

'Tis calm and still and almost drear
So utter is its solitude;
But still I love to linger here
And form my mood to nature's mood —

There's a wild walk beneath the rocks
Following the bend of Aspin side
'Tis worn by feet of mountain flocks
That wander down to drink the tide

Never by glen still and guarded river
Wound fairy path so sweet to me
Yet of the native shepherds nine
In open day and cheerful sun
Will tread its labyrinth alone

For here when evening's pensive hour
Hushes the bird and shuts the flower
And gives to Fancy magic power
O'er each familiar tone

For round their home the wanderers nightly tell the tale
And every listener swears it true
How wanderers there a phantom pale
With spirit eyes of dreamy blue —

It always walks with head declined
Its long curls move not in the wind

Its face is fair—divinely fair;
But brooding on that angel brow *
Rests such a shade of deep despair
As nought divine could ever know.

40 How oft in twilight, lingering lone,
I've stood to watch that phantom rise,
And seen in mist and moonlit stone
Its gleaming hair and solemn eyes.

The ancient men, in secret, say
'Tis the first chief of Aspin grey
That haunts his feudal home;
But why, around that alien grave
Three thousand miles beyond the wave,
Where his exiled ashes lie
50 Under the cope of England's sky,
Doth he not rather roam?

I've seen his picture in the hall;
It hangs upon an eastern wall,
And often when the sun declines
That picture like an angel shines;
And when the moonbeam, chill and blue,*
Streams the spectral windows through,
That picture's like a spectre too.

The hall is full of portraits rare;
60 Beauty and mystery mingle there:
At his right hand an infant fair
Looks from its golden frame;
And just like his its ringlets bright,
Its large dark eye of shadowy light,*
Its cheeks' pure hue, its forehead white,
And like its noble name.

Daughter divine! and could his gaze
Fall coldly on thy peerless face?

And did he never smile to see
70 Himself restored to infancy?

Never part back that golden flow *
Of curls, and kiss that pearly brow,
And feel no other earthly bliss
Was equal to that parent's kiss?

No; turn towards the western side:
There stands Sidonia's deity,
In all her glory, all her pride!
And truly like a god she seems:
Some god of wild enthusiast's dreams;
80 And this is she for whom he died:
For whom his spirit, unforgiven,
Wanders unsheltered, shut from heaven—
An outcast for eternity.

Those eyes are dust, those lips are clay;
That form is mouldered all away;
Nor thought, nor sense, nor pulse, nor breath:
The whole devoured and lost in death!

There is no worm, however mean,
That, living, is not nobler now
90 Than she, Lord Alfred's idol queen,
So loved, so worshipped, long ago.

O come away! the Norman door
Is silvered with a sudden shine;
Come, leave these dreams o'er things of yore
And turn to Nature's face divine.

O'er wood and wold, o'er flood and fell,
O'er flashing lake and gleaming dell,
The harvest moon looks down;
And when heaven smiles with love and light,*

100 And earth looks back so dazzling bright—
       In such a scene, on such a night,*
       Earth's children should not frown.

This poem appears to have been commenced in Brussels and finished
after the author returned home to Haworth Parsonage.

A20

155.   October 23, 1842—February 6, 1843

       The evening passes fast away,
       'Tis almost time to rest;
       What thoughts has left the vanished day?
       What feelings in thy breast?

       "The vanished day? It leaves a sense
       Of labour hardly done;
       Of little gained with vast expense—
       A sense of grief alone!

       "Time stands before the door of Death,
       Upbraiding bitterly;
       And Conscience, with exhaustless breath,
       Pours black reproach on me:

       "And though I think that Conscience lies,*
       And Time should Fate condemn;
       Still, weak Repentance clouds my eyes,*
       And makes me yield to them!"

       Then art thou glad to seek repose?
       Art glad to leave the sea,
       And anchor all thy weary woes
       In calm Eternity?

Nothing regrets to see thee go—
Not one voice sobs, "Farewell";
And where thy heart has suffered so
Canst thou desire to dwell?

"Alas! the countless links are strong
That bind us to our clay;
The loving spirit lingers long,
And would not pass away—

"And rest is sweet, when laurelled fame
Will crown the soldier's crest;
But a brave heart with a tarnished name
Would rather fight than rest."

Well, thou hast fought for many a year,
Hast fought thy whole life through,
Hast humbled Falsehood, trampled Fear;
What is there left to do?

" 'Tis true, this arm has hotly striven,
Has dared what few would dare;
Much have I done, and freely given,
Yet little learnt to bear!" *

Look on the grave where thou must sleep,
Thy last and strongest foe;
'Twill be endurance not to weep *
If that repose be woe.*

The long fight closing in defeat—*
Defeat serenely borne—
Thine eventide may still be sweet,*
Thy night a glorious morn.*

Commenced in Brussels a fortnight before the author left for home on account of the death of her aunt and foster-mother, Miss Elizabeth Branwell.

G123

SELF-INTERROGATION

"The evening passes fast away
Line 13 "And though I've said that Conscience lies
15 Still, sad Repentance clouds my eyes
40 But little learnt to bear
43 It is endurance not to weep
44 If that repose seem woe
45 The long war closing in defeat
47 Thy midnight rest may still be sweet
48 And break in glorious morn

B20

156. E.J.   February 24, 1843
ON THE FALL OF ZALONA [1]

All blue and bright, in glorious light,*
The morn comes marching on;
And now Zalona's steeples white
Glow golden in the sun.

This day might be a festal day:
The streets are crowded all;
And emerald flags stream broad and gay [2]
From turret, tower, and wall.

And, hark! how music evermore
10 Is sounding in the sky:
The deep bells boom, the cannon roar,
The trumpets sound on high—

The deep bells boom, the deep bells clash,
Upon the reeling air;

[1] The capital city of the Kingdom of Zalona, in the island of Gaaldine.
[2] The green standard flags of Gerald Exina, King of Zalona.

The cannon with unceasing crash
Make answer far and near.

What do those brazen tongues proclaim,
What joyous fête begun?
What offering to our country's fame,
20   What noble victory won?

Go, ask that solitary sire,
Laid in his house alone,
His silent hearth without a fire
His sons and daughters gone.

Go, ask those children in the street,
Beside their mother's door,
Waiting to hear the lingering feet
That they shall hear no more.

Ask those pale soldiers round the gates,
30   With famine-kindled eye:
They'll say, "Zalona celebrates *
The day that she must die."

The charger, by his manger tied,
Has rested many a day; *
Yet, ere the spur have touched his side,*
Behold, he sinks away!

And hungry dogs, with wolf-like cry,
Unburied corpses tear,
While their gaunt masters gaze and sigh
40   And scarce the feast forbear.

Now, look down from Zalona's wall—
There war the unwearied foe;
If ranks before our cannon fall,*
New ranks for ever grow.

And many a week, unbroken thus
Their troops our ramparts hem;
And for each man that fights for us,
A hundred fight for them!

Courage and Right and spotless Truth
50 Were pitched 'gainst trait'rous crime;
We offered all—our age, our youth,
Our brave men in their prime—

And all have failed—the fervent prayers;
The trust in heavenly aid;
Valour and Faith and sealèd tears
That would not mourn the dead;

Lips, that did breathe no murmuring word;
Hearts, that did ne'er complain,
Though vengeance held a sheathèd sword,
60 And martyrs bled in vain.

Alas, alas, the Myrtle bowers
By blighting blasts destroyed!
Alas, the Lily's withered flowers
That leave the garden void! *

Unfolds o'er tower, and waves o'er height,
A sheet of crimson [1] sheen:
Is it the setting sun's red light
That stains our standard green?

Heaven help us in this awful hour!
70 For now might Faith decay—
Now might we doubt God's guardian power
And curse instead of pray.

[1] The crimson standard of Julius Brenzaida, King of Angora in Gondal, and of Almedore in Gaaldine. See No. 40.

He will not even let us die—
Not let us die at home;
The foe must see our soldiers fly
As they had feared the tomb;

Because we *dare* not stay to gain
Those longed-for, glorious graves—
We dare not shrink from slavery's chain
80　To leave our children slaves!

But when this scene of awful woe
Has neared its final close,
As God forsook our armies, so
May He forsake our foes!

A23

157.　　　HOW CLEAR SHE SHINES!　　April 13, 1843

How clear she shines! How quietly
I lie beneath her silver light *
While Heaven and Earth are whispering me,
"To-morrow wake, but dream to-night."

Yes, Fancy, come, my Fairy love!
These throbbing temples, softly kiss;
And bend my lonely couch above
And bring me rest and bring me bliss.

The world is going—Dark world, adieu!
Grim world, go hide thee till the day; *
The heart thou canst not all subdue
Must still resist if thou delay!

Thy love I will not, will not share;
Thy hatred only wakes a smile;
Thy griefs may wound—thy wrongs may tear,
But, oh, thy lies shall ne'er beguile!

While gazing on the stars that glow
Above me in that stormless sea,
I long to hope that all the woe
Creation knows, is held in thee!

And this shall be my dream to-night—
I'll think the heaven of glorious spheres
Is rolling on its course of light
In endless bliss through endless years;

I'll think there's not one world above,
Far as these straining eyes can see,
Where Wisdom ever laughed at Love,
Or Virtue crouched to Infamy;

Where, writhing 'neath the strokes of Fate,
The mangled wretch was forced to smile;
To match his patience 'gainst her hate,
His heart rebellious all the while;

Where Pleasure still will lead to wrong,
And helpless Reason warn in vain;
And Truth is weak and Treachery strong,
And Joy the shortest path to Pain; *

And Peace, the lethargy of grief;
And Hope, a phantom of the soul;
And Life, a labour void and brief;
And Death, the despot of the whole!

G103

HOW CLEAR SHE SHINES!

How clear she shines! how quietly
Line 2 I lie beneath her guardian light
    10 Grim world, conceal thee till the day
    36 And Joy the surest path to Pain

B26

158.   TO A.S., 1830   E.   May 1, 1843

Where beams the sun the brightest
In the noons of sweet July? *
Where falls the snow the lightest
From bleak December's sky?

Where can the weary lay his head,
And lay it safe the while *
In a grave that never shuts its dead
From heaven's benignant smile?

Upon the earth in sunlight *
Spring grass grows green and fair;
But beneath the earth is midnight,
Eternal midnight there.

Then why lament that those we love
Escape Earth's dungeon tomb?
As if the flowers that blow above
Could charm its undergloom?

From morning's faintest dawning
Till evening's deepest shade,
Thou wilt not cease thy mourning
To know where she is laid.

But if to weep above her grave
Be such a priceless boon,
Go, shed thy tears in Ocean's wave
And they will reach it soon.

Yet, midst thy wild repining—
Mad though that anguish be—

Think heaven on her is shining,
Even as it shines on thee.

With thy mind's vision pierce the deep;
Look how she rests below;
And tell me why such blessèd sleep
Should cause such bitter woe?

The transcript of this poem made by the Reverend A. B. Nicholls has
the title "Grave in the Ocean" in place of the manuscript heading.

B25

159.   E.G. to M.R.   E.   May 4, 1843

Thy Guardians are asleep,
So I've come to bid thee rise:
Thou hast a holy vow to keep
Ere yon crescent quit the skies.

Though clouds careering wide
Will hardly let her gleam,
She's bright enough to be our guide
Across the mountain-stream.

O waken, Dearest, wake!
What means this long delay?
Say, wilt thou not for honour's sake *
Chase idle fears away?

Think not of future grief
Entailed on present joy:
An age of woe were only brief
Its memory to destroy.

And neither Hell nor Heaven,
Though both conspire at last,
Can take the bliss that has been given,
Can rob us of the past.

Then, waken, Mary, wake:
How canst thou linger now?
For true love's and Gleneden's sake,*
Arise and keep thy vow.

Under the heading to this poem in the manuscript, Charlotte Brontë
has written "A Serenade"; above "honour's" in line 11 she has written
"true love's"; and above "Gleneden's" in line 23 she has written "for
honour's."

D8

160.   It was night, and on the mountains
       Fathoms deep the snow-drifts lay;
       Streams and waterfalls and fountains
       Down in darkness stole away.*

       Long ago the hopeless peasant
       Left his sheep all buried there:
       Sheep that through the summer pleasant
       He had watched with fondest care.*

       Now no more a cheerful ranger
       Following pathways known of yore,
       Sad he stood a wildered stranger *
       On his own unbounded moor.

Between the first and second verses there are four cancelled lines in
the manuscript:

       Cold and wild the wind was blowing
       Keen and clear the heaven above,
       But though countless stars were glowing
       Absent was the star of love.

161.   Had there been falsehood in my breast
       No thorns had marred my road,*

This spirit had not lost its rest,
These tears had never flowed.

July 26, 1843 [1]

Manuscript D8 is a separate leaf, with Nos. 160, 161, and two verses
of No. 110 on one side, and on the other side No. 162:

162.   Yes, holy be thy resting place
       Wherever thou may'st lie;
       The sweetest winds breathe on thy face,
       The softest of the sky.

       And will not guardian Angels send
       Kind dreams and thoughts of love,
       Though I no more may watchful bend
       Thy longed repose above? *

       And will not heaven itself bestow
       A beam of glory there
       That summer's grass more green may grow,
       And summer's flowers more fair?

       Farewell, farewell, 'tis hard to part
       Yet, loved one, it must be:
       I would not rend another heart
       Not even by blessing thee.

       Go! we must break affection's chain,
       Forget the hopes of years:
       Nay, grieve not—willest thou remain *
       To waken wilder tears?

       This wild [2] breeze with thee and me *
       Roved in the dawning day; *
       And thou shouldest be where it shall be *
       Ere evening, far away.

[1] The figure "3" is indistinct in the manuscript, and may be meant for "2."
[2] Or "herald."

B27

163.   E.   September 6, 1843

In the earth, the earth, thou shalt be laid,
A grey stone standing over thee;
Black mould beneath thee spread
And black mould to cover thee.

"Well, there is rest there,
So fast come thy prophecy;
The time when my sunny hair
Shall with grass roots twinèd be." *

But cold, cold is that resting place,
Shut out from Joy and Liberty,
And all who loved thy living face
Will shrink from its gloom and thee.*

"Not so: *here* the world is chill,
And sworn friends fall from me;
But *there,* they'll own me still *
And prize my memory."

Farewell, then, all that love,
All that deep sympathy:
Sleep on; heaven laughs above,
Earth never misses thee.

Turf-sod and tombstone drear
Part human company;
One heart broke only there—*
That heart was worthy thee! *

Pencilled on the manuscript in Charlotte Brontë's handwriting are
the title "Warning and Reply" and the differences in the text of the
poem as printed in 1850.

H483

WARNING AND REPLY

In the earth—the earth—thou shalt be laid
Line 8 Shall with grass roots entwined be
  12 Will shrink from it shudderingly
  15 But *there*—they will own me still
  23 One heart breaks only—here
  24 But that heart was worthy thee!

B38

164. RODRIC LESLEY. 1830 Dec. 18, 1843

Lie down and rest—the fight is done,
Thy comrades to the camp retire;
Gaze not so earnestly upon
The far gleam of the beacon fire.

Listen not to the wind-borne sounds *
Of music and of soldiers' cheer;
Thou canst not go—unnumbered wounds
Exhaust thy life and hold thee here.

Had that hand power to raise the sword,
Which since this morn laid hundreds low; *
Had that tongue strength to speak the word
That urged thy followers on the foe:

Were that warm blood within thy veins,
Which now upon the earth is flowing,
Splashing its sod with crimson stains,
Reddening the pale heath round thee growing;

Then, Rodric, thou might'st still be turning
With eager eye and anxious breast

To where those signal-lights are burning—
To where thy monarch's legions rest.*

But, never more! Look up and see
The twilight fading from the skies:
That last dim beam that sets for thee,
Rodric, for thee shall never rise!

In the manuscript the name "Roderic" has been written in pencil by
Charlotte Brontë below the title; and "war-worn comrades" above
"monarch's legions" in line 20.

A21

165.   HOPE   December 18, 1843

Hope was but a timid friend;
She sat without my grated den,*
Watching how my fate would tend,
Even as selfish-hearted men.

She was cruel in her fear;
Through the bars, one dreary day,
I looked out to see her there,
And she turned her face away!

Like a false guard, false watch keeping,
Still, in strife, she whispered peace;
She would sing while I was weeping;
When [1] I listened, she would cease.*

False she was, and unrelenting;
When my last joys strewed the ground,
Even Sorrow saw, repenting,
Those sad relics scattered round;

[1] Or "if."

Hope—whose whisper would have given
Balm to all that frenzied pain—*
Stretched her wings and soared to heaven;
Went—and ne'er returned again!

G82

HOPE

Hope was but a timid friend
Line 2 She sat without the grated den
12 If I listened, she would cease
18 Balm to all my frenzied pain

B29

166. M.G. FOR THE U.S.[1]   December 19, 1843

'Twas yesterday, at early dawn,
I watched the falling snow;
A drearier scene on winter morn
Was never stretched below.

I could not see the mountains round,
But I knew by the wild wind's roar
How every drift, in their glens profound,
Was deepening ever more.

And then I thought of Ula's bowers
Beyond the southern sea;
Her tropic prairies bright with flowers
And rivers wandering free.

I thought of many a happy day
Spent in her Eden isle,
With my dear comrades, young and gay,
All scattered now so far away,
But not forgot the while!

[1] "Unique Society" (see page 234).

Who that has breathed that heavenly air,
To northern climes would come,
To Gondal's mists and moorlands drear,
And sleet and frozen gloom?

Spring brings the swallow and the lark:
But what will winter bring?
Its twilight noons and evenings dark *
To match the gifts of spring? *

No! Look with me o'er that sullen main: *
If thy spirit's eye can see,*
There are brave ships floating back again
That no calm southern port could chain *
From Gondal's stormy sea.

O how the hearts of the voyagers beat *
To feel the frost-wind blow!
What flower in Ula's gardens sweet *
Is worth one flake of snow?

The blast which almost rends their sail
Is welcome as a friend;
It brings them home, that thundering gale,
Home to their journey's end;

Home to our souls whose wearying sighs
Lament their absence drear,
And feel how bright even winter skies *
Would shine if they were here!

A transcript of this poem, made by the Reverend A. B. Nicholls, has the title "North and South" in place of the manuscript heading.

E20

167.   A.S.   CASTLE WOOD   February 2, 1844

The day is done, the winter sun
Is setting in its sullen sky;

And drear the course that has been run,
And dim the beams that slowly die.*

No star will light my coming night;
No moon of hope for me will shine; *
I mourn not heaven would blast my sight,
And I never longed for ways divine.*

Through Life hard Task I did not ask *
Celestial aid, celestial cheer;
I saw my fate without its mask,
And met it too without a tear.

The grief that prest this living breast *
Was heavier far than earth can be;
And who would dread eternal rest
When labour's hire was agony? *

Dark falls the fear of this despair
On spirits born for happiness; *
But I was bred the mate of care,
The foster-child of sore distress.

No sighs for me, no sympathy,
No wish to keep my soul below;
The heart is dead since infancy,*
Unwept-for let the body go.[1]

A22

168.   MY COMFORTER   February 10, 1844

Well hast thou spoken—and yet not taught
A feeling strange or new;
Thou hast but roused a latent thought,

[1] In the manuscript this line is substituted for

Unmourned, the body well may go.

A cloud-closed beam of sunshine brought
To gleam in open view.

Deep down—concealed within my soul,
That light lies hid from men,
Yet glows unquenched—though shadows roll,
Its gentle ray can not control—
About the sullen den.

Was I not vexed, in these gloomy ways
To walk unlit so long? *
Around me, wretches uttering praise,
Or howling o'er their hopeless days,
And each with Frenzy's tongue—

A Brotherhood of misery,
With smiles as sad as sighs; *
Their madness daily maddening me,*
And turning into agony *
The Bliss before my eyes.

So stood I, in Heaven's glorious sun
And in the glare of Hell
My spirit drank a mingled tone
Of seraph's song and demon's moan—
What my soul bore my soul alone
Within its self may tell.*

Like a soft air above a sea
Tossed by the tempest's stir—
A thaw-wind melting quietly
The snowdrift on some wintery lea;
No—what sweet thing can match with thee,*
My thoughtful Comforter?

And yet a little longer speak,
Calm this resentful mood,

And while the savage heart grows meek,
For other token do not seek,
But let the tear upon my cheek
Evince my gratitude.

G153

MY COMFORTER

Well hast thou spoken, and yet not taught
Line 12 To walk alone so long
17 Their smiles as sad as sighs
18 Whose madness daily maddened me
19 Distorting into agony
31 No: what sweet thing resembles thee

B5

169. A.G.A. TO A.S.   E.   March 2, 1844

This summer wind, with thee and me
Roams in the dawn of day;
But thou must be where it shall be,
Ere Evening—far away.[1]

The farewell's echo from thy soul
Should not depart before
Hills rise and distant rivers roll
Between us evermore.

I know that I have done thee wrong—
Have wronged both thee and Heaven—
And I may mourn my lifetime long
Yet may not be forgiven.

[1] A variation of the last stanza of No. 162.

Repentant tears will vainly fall
To cancel deeds untrue; *
But for no grief can I recall
The dreary word—Adieu.

Yet thou a future peace shalt win
Because thy soul is clear;
And I who had the heart to sin
Will find a heart to bear.

Till far beyond earth's frenzied strife
That makes destruction joy,
Thy perished faith shall spring to life
And my remorse shall die.

A24

170.   A DAY DREAM   March 5, 1844

On a sunny brae alone I lay
One summer afternoon;
It was the marriage-time of May
With her young lover, June.

From her Mother's heart seemed loath to part
That queen of bridal charms,
But her Father smiled on the fairest child
He ever held in his arms.

The trees did wave their plumy crests,
10 The glad birds carolled clear;
And I, of all the wedding guests,
Was only sullen there.

There was not one but wished to shun
My aspect void of cheer;

The very grey rocks, looking on,
Asked, "What do you do here?" *

And I could utter no reply:
In sooth I did not know
Why I had brought a clouded eye
20 To greet the general glow.

So, resting on a heathy bank,
I took my heart to me;
And we together sadly sank
Into a reverie.

We thought, "When winter comes again,
Where will these bright things be?
All vanished, like a vision vain,
An unreal mockery!

"The birds that now so blithely sing,
30 Through deserts frozen dry,
Poor spectres of the perished Spring
In famished troops will fly.

"And why should we be glad at all?
The leaf is hardly green,
Before a token of the fall *
Is on its surface seen." *

Now whether it were really so
I never could be sure;
But as, in fit of peevish woe,
40 I stretched me on the moor,

A thousand thousand glancing fires *
Seemed kindling in the air;
A thousand thousand silvery lyres
Resounded far and near:

Methought the very breath I breathed
Was full of sparks divine,
And all my heather-couch was wreathed
By that celestial shine.

And while the wide Earth echoing rang *
50 To their strange minstrelsy,*
The little glittering spirits sang,*
Or seemed to sing, to me:

"O mortal, mortal, let them die;
Let Time and Tears destroy,
That we may overflow the sky
With universal joy.

"Let Grief distract the sufferer's breast,
And Night obscure his way;
They hasten him to endless rest,
60 And everlasting day.

"To Thee the world is like a tomb,
A desert's naked shore;
To us, in unimagined bloom,
It brightens more and more.

"And could we lift the veil and give
One brief glimpse to thine eye
Thou would'st rejoice for those that live,
Because they live to die." *

The music ceased—the noonday Dream
70 Like dream of night withdrew
But Fancy still will sometimes deem
Her fond creation true.

G89

A DAY DREAM

On a sunny brae alone I lay
Line 16 Asked, "What do you here?"
   35 Before a token of its fall
   36 Is on the surface seen
   41 A thousand thousand gleaming fires
   49 And, while the wide earth echoing rung
   50 To that strange minstrelsy
   51 The little glittering spirits sung
   68 *Because* they live to die."

B23

171. E.   E.W. TO A.G.A.   March 11, 1844

How few, of all the hearts that loved,
Are grieving for thee now!
And why should mine, to-night, be moved
With such a sense of woe?

Too often, thus, when left alone
Where none my thoughts can see,
Comes back a word, a passing tone
From thy strange history.

Sometimes I seem to see thee rise,
A glorious child again—
All virtues beaming from thine eyes
That ever honoured men—

Courage and Truth, a generous breast
Where Love and Gladness lay; *
A being whose very Memory blest *
And made the mourner gay.*

O, fairly spread thy early sail,
And fresh and pure and free
Was the first impulse of the gale
That urged life's wave for thee! *

Why did the pilot, too confiding,
Dream o'er that Ocean's foam,
And trust in Pleasure's careless guiding
To bring his vessel home?

For well he knew what dangers frowned,
What mists would gather dim;
What rocks and shelves and sands lay round
Between his port and him.

The very brightness of the sun,
The splendour of the main,
The wind that bore him wildly on *
Should not have warned in vain.

An anxious gazer from the shore,
I marked the whitening wave,
And wept above thy fate the more
Because I could not save.

It recks not now, when all is over;
But yet my heart will be
A mourner still, though friend and lover
Have both forgotten thee!

Beneath the heading in this manuscript, Charlotte Brontë has written,
"On a life perverted." In preparing the poem for publication in 1850 she
gave it the title "The Wanderer from the Fold," and made several alterations in the text. It is now seen from the author's date and heading to
the poem that it does *not* refer to Patrick Branwell Brontë, as hitherto
supposed. He died on September 24, 1848.

H482

THE WANDERER FROM THE FOLD

How few, of all the hearts that loved
Line 14 Where sinless sunshine lay:
    15 A being whose very presence blest
    16 Like gladsome summer-day.
    20 Which urged life's wave for thee
    31 The wind which bore him wildly on

B24

172. Come, walk with me;
    There's only thee
    To bless my spirit now;
    We used to love on winter nights
    To wander through the snow.
    Can we not woo back old delights?
    The clouds rush dark and wild;
    They fleck with shade our mountain heights *
    The same as long ago,
    And on the horizon rest at last
    In looming masses piled;
    While moonbeams flash and fly so fast
    We scarce can say they smiled.

    Come, walk with me—come, walk with me;
    We were not once so few;
    But Death has stolen our company
    As sunshine steals the dew:
    He took them one by one, and we
    Are left, the only two;
    So closer would my feelings twine,
    Because they have no stay but thine.

"Nay, call me not; it may not be;
Is human love so true?
Can Friendship's flower droop on for years *
And then revive anew?
No; though the soil be wet with tears,
How fair soe'er it grew;
The vital sap once perishèd
Will never flow again;
And surer than that dwelling dread,
The narrow dungeon of the dead,
Time parts the hearts of men."

B30

173.   May 1, 1844

The linnet in the rocky dells,
The moor-lark in the air,
The bee among the heather-bells
That hide my lady fair:

The wild deer browse above her breast;
The wild birds raise their brood;
And they, her smiles of love caressed,
Have left her solitude!

I ween, that when the grave's dark wall
Did first her form retain,
They thought their hearts could ne'er recall
The light of joy again.

They thought the tide of grief would flow
Unchecked through future years,
But where is all their anguish now,
And where are all their tears?

Well, let them fight for Honour's breath,
Or Pleasure's shade pursue—
The Dweller in the land of Death
Is changed and careless too.

And if their eyes should watch and weep
Till sorrow's source were dry,
She would not, in her tranquil sleep,
Return a single sigh.

Blow, west wind, by the lonely mound,
And murmur, summer streams,
There is no need of other sound
To soothe my Lady's dreams.

                                E.W.

G43

SONG

The linnet in the rocky dells
The printed text agrees with the manuscript.

A25

174.   TO IMAGINATION   September 3, 1844

When weary with the long day's care,
And earthly change from pain to pain,
And lost, and ready to despair,
Thy kind voice calls me back again—
O my true friend, I am not lone
While thou canst speak with such a tone!

So hopeless is the world without,
The world within I doubly prize;
Thy world where guile and hate and doubt

And cold suspicion never rise;
Where thou and I and Liberty
Have undisputed sovereignty.

What matters it that all around
Danger and grief and darkness lie,*
If but within our bosom's bound
We hold a bright unsullied sky,*
Warm with ten thousand mingled rays
Of suns that know no winter days?

Reason indeed may oft complain
For Nature's sad reality,
And tell the suffering heart how vain
Its cherished dreams must always be;
And Truth may rudely trample down
The flowers of Fancy newly blown.

But thou art ever there to bring
The hovering visions back and breathe *
New glories o'er the blighted spring
And call a lovelier life from death,
And whisper with a voice divine
Of real worlds as bright as thine.

I trust not to thy phantom bliss,
Yet still in evening's quiet hour
With never-failing thankfulness
I welcome thee, benignant power,
Sure solacer of human cares
And brighter hope when hope despairs.*

G96

TO IMAGINATION

When weary with the long day's care
Line 14 Danger, and guilt, and darkness lie

16 We hold a bright, untroubled sky
26 The hovering vision back, and breathe
36 And sweeter hope, when hope despairs

B33

175.   E.   D.G.C. to J.A.   October 2, 1844

Come, the wind may never again
Blow as now it blows for us;
And the stars may never again shine as now they shine;
Long before October returns,
Seas of blood will have parted us;
And you must crush the love in your heart, and I the love
  in mine!

For face to face will our kindred stand,
And as they are so shall we be;
Forgetting how the same sweet earth has borne and nour-
  ished all—
One must fight for the people's power,
And one for the rights of Royalty;
And each be ready to give his life to work the other's fall.

The chance of war we cannot shun,
Nor would we shrink from our fathers' cause,
Nor dread Death more because the hand that gives it may
  be dear;
We must bear to see Ambition rule
Over Love, with his iron laws;
Must yield our blood for a stranger's sake, and refuse our-
  selves a tear!

So, the wind may never again
Blow as now it blows for us,
And the stars may never again shine as now they shine;
Next October, the cannon's roar

From hostile ranks may be urging us—
Me to strike for your life's blood, and you to strike for mine.

Now printed for the first time in an edition of the poems, but see page 35.

A26

176.   October 14, 1844

O thy bright eyes must answer now,
When Reason, with a scornful brow,
Is mocking at my overthrow;
O thy sweet tongue must plead for me
And tell why I have chosen thee!

Stern Reason is to judgement come
Arrayed in all her forms of gloom:
Wilt thou my advocate be dumb?
No, radiant angel, speak and say
Why I did cast the world away;

Why I have persevered to shun
The common paths that others run;
And on a strange road journeyed on
Heedless alike of Wealth and Power—
Of Glory's wreath and Pleasure's flower.

These once indeed seemed Beings divine,
And they perchance heard vows of mine
And saw my offerings on their shrine—
But, careless gifts are seldom prized,
And mine were worthily despised; *

So with a ready heart I swore
To seek their altar-stone no more,
And gave my spirit to adore
Thee, ever present, phantom thing—
My slave, my comrade, and my King!

A slave because I rule thee still;
Incline thee to my changeful will
And make thy influence good or ill—
A comrade, for by day and night
Thou art my intimate delight—

My Darling Pain that wounds and sears
And wrings a blessing out from tears
By deadening me to real cares; *
And yet, a king—though prudence well
Have taught thy subject to rebel.

And am I wrong to worship where
Faith cannot doubt nor Hope despair
Since my own soul can grant my prayer?
Speak, God of Visions, plead for me
And tell why I have chosen thee!

G118

PLEAD FOR ME

Oh, thy bright eyes must answer now
Line 20 And *mine* were worthily despised
33 By deadening me to earthly cares

B34

177.   I.M. TO I.G.   November 6, 1844

"The winter wind is loud and wild;
Come close to me, my darling child!
Forsake thy books and mateless play,
And, while the night is closing grey,*
We'll talk its pensive hours away—

"Iernë, round our sheltered hall,
November's blasts unheeded call; *

Not one faint breath can enter here
Enough to wave my daughter's hair;

10 "And I am glad to watch the blaze
Glance from her eyes, with mimic rays;
To feel her cheek so softly pressed
In happy quiet on my breast;

"But, yet, even this tranquillity
Brings bitter, restless thoughts to me;
And, in the red fire's cheerful glow,
I think of deep glens, blocked with snow;

"I dream of moor, and misty hill,
Where evening gathers, dark and chill,*
20 For, lone, among the mountains cold
Lie those that I have loved of old,
And my heart aches, in speechless pain,*
Exhausted with repinings vain,
That I shall see them ne'er again!" *

"Father, in early infancy,
When you were far beyond the sea,
Such thoughts were tyrants over me—
I often sat for hours together,
Through the long nights of angry weather,
30 Raised on my pillow, to descry
The dim moon struggling in the sky;
Or, with strained ear, to catch the shock
Of rock with wave, and wave with rock.
So would I fearful vigil keep,
And, all for listening, never sleep;
But this world's life has much to dread:
Not so, my father, with the Dead.

"O not for them should we despair;
The grave is drear, but they are not there:
40 Their dust is mingled with the sod;

Their happy souls are gone to God!
You told me this, and yet you sigh,
And murmur that your friends must die.
Ah, my dear father, tell me why?

"For, if your former words were true,
How useless would such sorrow be!
As wise to mourn the seed which grew
Unnoticed on its parent tree,

"Because it fell in fertile earth
50 And sprang up to a glorious birth—
Struck deep its roots, and lifted high *
Its green boughs in the breezy sky!

"But I'll not fear—I will not weep
For those whose bodies lie asleep: *
I know there is a blessed shore
Opening its ports for me and mine;
And, gazing Time's wide waters o'er,
I weary for that land divine,

"Where we were born—where you and I
60 Shall meet our dearest, when we die;
From suffering and corruption free,
Restored into the Deity."

"Well hast thou spoken, sweet, trustful child!
And wiser than thy sire:
And coming tempests, raging wild,*
Shall strengthen thy desire—
Thy fervent hope, through storm and foam,
Through wind and Ocean's roar,
To reach, at last, the eternal home—
70 The steadfast, changeless shore!"

G8

FAITH AND DESPONDENCY

"The winter wind is loud and wild
Line 4 And, while the night is gathering gray
     7 November's gusts unheeded call
  19 Where evening closes dark and chill
  22 And my heart aches, in hopeless pain
  24 That I shall greet them ne'er again
  51 Struck deep its root, and lifted high
  54 For those whose bodies rest in sleep
  65 And worldly tempests, raging wild

B31

178. E.J.B., Nov. 11, 1844   J.B., Sept., 1825

FROM A DUNGEON WALL IN
THE SOUTHERN COLLEGE

"Listen! when your hair, like mine,
Takes a tint of silver grey;
When your eyes, with dimmer shine,
Watch life's bubbles float away;

"When you, young man, have borne like me,
The weary weight of sixty-three,
Then shall penance sore be paid
For these hours so wildly squandered; *
And the words that now fall dead
10 On your ears, be deeply pondered; *
Pondered and approved at last,
But their virtue will be past!

"Glorious is the prize of Duty,
Though she be a serious power; *

Treacherous all the lures of Beauty,
Thorny bud and poisonous flower!

"Mirth is but a mad beguiling
Of the golden-gifted Time;
Love, a demon-meteor, wiling
20 Heedless feet to gulfs of crime.

"Those who follow earthly pleasure,
Heavenly knowledge will not lead;
Wisdom hides from them her treasure,
Virtue bids them evil-speed!

"Vainly may their hearts, repenting,
Seek for aid in future years;
Wisdom scorned knows no relenting;
Virtue is not won by tears.*

"Fain would we your steps reclaim,
30 Waken fear and holy shame.
And to this end, our council well
And kindly doomed you to a cell
Whose darkness may, perchance, disclose
A beacon-guide from sterner woes."

So spake my judge—then seized his lamp
And left me in the dungeon damp,
A vault-like place whose stagnant air
Suggests and nourishes despair!

Rosina, this had never been
40 Except for you, my despot queen! *
Except for you the billowy sea
Would now be tossing under me,
The wind's wild voice my bosom thrill
And my glad heart bound wilder still,

Flying before the rapid gale
Those wondrous southern isles to hail
Which wait for my companions free
But thank your passion—not for me!

You know too well—and so do I—
50 Your haughty beauty's sovereignty;
Yet have I read those falcon eyes—
Have dived into their mysteries—
Have studied long their glance and feel
It is not love those eyes reveal.

They Flash, they burn with lightning shine,
But not with such fond fire as mine;
The tender star fades faint and wan
Before Ambition's scorching sun.
So deem I now—and Time will prove
60 If I have wronged Rosina's love.

Under the heading in the manuscript, Charlotte Brontë has written
"T[he] Old Man's lecture"; but she gave the title "The Elder's Rebuke" to that part of the poem (lines 1 to 28) which she selected for
printing in 1850, and added 6 lines which are not in the manuscript.

The last four verses have been printed as a separate poem. They appear separately in the Reverend A. B. Nicholls's transcripts, with the title
"Love's Rebuke."

Lines 29 to 38 are now printed for the first time in an edition of the
poems, but see note on page 35.

H481

THE ELDER'S REBUKE

"Listen! When your hair, like mine
Line 8 For those hours so wildly squandered
10 On your ear, be deeply pondered
14 Though she be a "serious power"
28 Virtue is not won by fears

After line 28, the poem ends with 6 lines added by Charlotte Brontë:

> Thus spake the ice-blooded elder gray:
> The young man scoffed as he turned away,
> Turned to the call of a sweet lute's measure,
> Waked by the lightsome touch of pleasure:
> Had he ne'er met a gentler teacher,
> Woe had been wrought by that pitiless preacher.

B35

179.   November 21, 1844

M. DOUGLAS TO E.R. GLENEDEN

The moon is full this winter night;
The stars are clear though few;
And every window glistens bright
With leaves of frozen dew.

The sweet moon through your lattice gleams
And lights your room like day;
And there you pass in happy dreams
The peaceful hours away;

While I, with effort hardly quelling
10 The anguish in my breast,
Wander about the silent dwelling
And cannot think of rest.

The old clock in the gloomy hall
Ticks on from hour to hour,
And every time its measured call
Seems lingering slow and slower.

And O how slow that keen-eyed star
Has tracked the chilly grey!
What watching yet, how very far
20 The morning lies away!

Beside your chamber door I stand: *
Love, are you slumbering still?
My cold heart underneath my hand
Has almost ceased to thrill.

Bleak, bleak the east wind sobs and sighs
And drowns the turret bell
Whose sad note, undistinguished, dies
Unheard, like my farewell.

To-morrow Scorn will blight my name
30 And Hate will trample me—
Will load me with a coward's shame:
A Traitor's perjury!

False Friends will launch their venomed sneers; *
True Friends will wish me dead;
And I shall cause the bitterest tears
That you have ever shed.

The dark deeds of my outlawed race
Will then like virtues shine;
And men will pardon their disgrace,
40 Beside the guilt of mine;

For who forgives the accursed crime
Of dastard treachery?
Rebellion in its chosen time
May Freedom's champion be;

Revenge may stain a righteous sword,
It may be just to slay;
But, Traitor—Traitor—from that word *
All true breasts shrink away!

O I would give my heart to death,
50 To keep my honour fair:
Yet, I'll not give my inward Faith
My Honour's name to spare—*

Not even to keep your priceless love,
Dare I, Beloved, deceive;
This treason should the future prove:
Gleneden, then believe! *

I know the path I ought to go;
I follow fearlessly,
Enquiring not what deeper woe
60 Stern Duty stores for me.

So Foes pursue, and cold allies
Mistrust me, every one:
Let me be false in others' eyes
If faithful in my own.

G140

HONOUR'S MARTYR

The moon is full this winter night
Line 21 Without your chamber door I stand
33 False friends will launch their covert sneers
47 But, traitor, traitor—from *that* word
52 My honour's *name* to spare
56 Then, only then, believe!

B32

180. Dec. 2, 1844   A.G.A. [1]
                                                     Sept., 1826

FROM A D— W— IN THE N.C.[2]

O Day! He cannot die
When thou so fair art shining;

[1] Augusta G. Almeda.
[2] From a Dungeon Wall in the Northern College. A poem by Anne Brontë is headed: "Lines inscribed on the wall of a dungeon in the southern P. of I. [Palace of Instruction] by A.H. [Alexander Hybernia]," and signed and dated at the end "Alexander, April, 1826."

O Sun! in such a glorious sky
So tranquilly declining,

"He cannot leave thee now
While fresh west-winds are blowing,
And all around his youthful brow
Thy cheerful light is glowing!

"Elbë,[1] awake, awake! *
10 The golden evening gleams
Warm and bright on Arden's [2] lake,
Arouse thee from thy dreams!

"Beside thee, on my knee,
My dearest friend, I pray
That thou, to cross the eternal sea
Wouldst yet *one* hour delay! *

"I hear its billows roar,
I see them foaming high,
But no glimpse of a further shore
20 Has blessed my straining eye.

"Believe not what they urge
Of Eden isles beyond;
Turn back, from that tempestuous surge,
To thy own native land!

"It is not Death, but pain
That struggles in thy breast;
Nay, rally, Elbë, rouse again,*
I cannot let thee rest!

One long look, that sore reproved me
30 For the woe I could not bear—

[1] Probably Alexander, Lord of Elbë.
[2] Written over the name "Elnor's" in the manuscript.

One mute look of suffering moved me
To repent my useless prayer;

And with sudden check, the heaving
Of distraction passed away;
Not a sign of further grieving
Stirred my soul that awful day.

Paled at last, that sweet sun setting; *
Sank to peace the gentle breeze; *
Summer dews fell softly, wetting
40 Glen and glade, and silent trees.

Then his eyes began to weary,
Weighed beneath a mortal sleep;
And their light grew strangely dreary,*
Clouded, even as they would weep;

But they wept not, but they changed not,
Never moved and never closed;
Troubled still, and still they ranged not,
Wandered not, nor yet reposed!

So I knew that he was dying—
50 Stooped and raised his languid head—
Felt no breath and heard no sighing,
So, I knew that he was dead.

G40

A DEATH-SCENE

"*O Day! he cannot die*
Line 9 Edward, awake, awake—
16 Wouldst yet one hour delay
27 Nay, rally, Edward, rouse again
37 Paled, at length, the sweet sun setting
38 Sunk to peace the twilight breeze
43 And their orbs grew strangely dreary

A27

"Enough of Thought, Philosopher;
Too long hast thou been dreaming
Unlightened, in this chamber drear
While summer's sun is beaming—
Space-sweeping soul, what sad refrain
Concludes thy musings once again?

"O for the time when I shall sleep
Without identity,
And never care how rain may steep
10 *Or snow may cover me!*

"No promised Heaven, these wild Desires
Could all or half fulfil;
No threatened Hell, with quenchless fires,
Subdue this quenchless will!"

—So said I, and still say the same;
—Still to my Death will say—
Three Gods within this little frame
Are warring night and day.

Heaven could not hold them all, and yet
20 They all are held in me
And must be mine till I forget
My present entity.

O for the time when in my breast
Their struggles will be o'er;
O for the day when I shall rest,
And never suffer more!

"I saw a Spirit standing, Man,
Where thou dost stand—an hour ago;
And round his feet, three rivers ran
30 Of equal depth and equal flow—

"A Golden stream, and one like blood,
And one like Sapphire, seemed to be,
But where they joined their triple flood
It tumbled in an inky sea.

"The Spirit bent his dazzling gaze *
Down on that Ocean's gloomy night,*
Then—kindling all with sudden blaze,
The glad deep sparkled wide and bright—
White as the sun; far, far more fair
40 Than the divided sources were!" *

—And even for that Spirit, Seer,
I've watched and sought my lifetime long;
Sought Him in Heaven, Hell, Earth and Air,
An endless search—and always wrong!

Had I but seen his glorious eye
Once light the clouds that 'wilder me,
I ne'er had raised this coward cry
To cease to think and cease to be—

I ne'er had called oblivion blest,
50 Nor stretching eager hands to Death
Implored to change for lifeless rest *
This sentient soul, this living breath.

O let me die, that power and will
Their cruel strife may close,
And vanquished Good, victorious Ill *
Be lost in one repose.

"The Philosopher's conclusion" has been added in pencil, apparently
by the author, at the head of the poem in the manuscript.

The last two verses appear to have been added to the manuscript in substitution for the following verse which is cancelled therein:

> O for the lid that cannot weep,
> The Breast that needs no breath—
> The tomb that brings eternal sleep—
> For Life's Deliverer, Death!

G23

THE PHILOSOPHER

Enough of thought, philosopher
Lines 7 to 14 are not in italics.
Line 35 The spirit sent his dazzling gaze
    36 Down through that ocean's gloomy night
    40 Than its divided sources were!
    51 Implored to change for senseless rest
    55 And conquered good and conquering ill

B36

182.   March 3, 1845

R. ALCONA TO J. BRENZAIDA [1]

Cold in the earth, and the deep snow piled above thee!
Far, far removed, cold in the dreary grave!
Have I forgot, my Only Love, to love thee,
Severed at last by Time's all-wearing wave?

Now, when alone, do my thoughts no longer hover
Over the mountains on Angora's shore;
Resting their wings where heath and fern-leaves cover
That noble heart for ever, ever more?

Cold in the earth, and fifteen wild Decembers
From those brown hills have melted into spring—

[1] Rosina Alcona to Julius Brenzaida.

Faithful indeed is the spirit that remembers
After such years of change and suffering!

Sweet Love of youth, forgive if I forget thee
While the World's tide is bearing me along:
Sterner desires and darker hopes beset me,
Hopes which obscure but cannot do thee wrong.

No other Sun has lightened up my heaven;
No other Star has ever shone for me:
All my life's bliss from thy dear life was given—
All my life's bliss is in the grave with thee.

But when the days of golden dreams had perished
And even Despair was powerless to destroy,
Then did I learn how existence could be cherished,
Strengthened and fed without the aid of joy;

Then did I check the tears of useless passion,
Weaned my young soul from yearning after thine;
Sternly denied its burning wish to hasten
Down to that tomb already more than mine!

And even yet, I dare not let it languish,
Dare not indulge in Memory's rapturous pain;
Once drinking deep of that divinest anguish,
How could I seek the empty world again?

G31

REMEMBRANCE

Cold in the earth—and the deep snow piled above thee
Line 4 Severed at last by Time's all-severing wave
    6 Over the mountains, on that northern shore
    8 Thy noble heart for ever, ever more
  15 Other desires and other hopes beset me
  17 No later light has lightened up my heaven,
  18 No second morn has ever shone for me

A29

183.   April 10, 1845

Death, that struck when I was most confiding
In my certain Faith of Joy to be,
Strike again, Time's withered branch dividing
From the fresh root of Eternity!

Leaves, upon Time's branch, were growing brightly,
Full of sap and full of silver dew;
Birds, beneath its shelter, gathered nightly;
Daily, round its flowers, the wild bees flew.

Sorrow passed and plucked the golden blossom,
Guilt stripped off the foliage in its pride;
But, within its parent's kindly bosom,
Flowed forever Life's restoring tide.

Little mourned I for the parted Gladness,
For the vacant nest and silent song;
Hope was there and laughed me out of sadness,
Whispering, "Winter will not linger long."

And behold, with tenfold increase blessing
Spring adorned the beauty-burdened spray;
Wind and rain and fervent heat caressing
Lavished glory on its second May.*

High it rose; no wingèd grief could sweep it;
Sin was scared to distance with its shine:
Love and its own life had power to keep it
From all wrong, from every blight but thine!

Heartless [1] Death, the young leaves droop and languish! *
Evening's gentle air may still restore—

[1] Or "Cruel."

No: the morning sunshine mocks my anguish—
Time for me must never blossom more!

Strike it down, that other boughs may flourish
Where that perished sapling used to be;
Thus, at least, its mouldering corpse will nourish
That from which it sprung—Eternity.

G128

DEATH

Death, that struck when I was most confiding
Line 20 Lavished glory on that second May
25 Cruel Death! The young leaves droop and languish

A28

184.   April 14, 1845

Ah! why, because the dazzling sun
Restored my earth to joy *
Have you departed, every one,
And left a desert sky?

All through the night, your glorious eyes
Were gazing down in mine,
And with a full heart's thankful sighs
I blessed that watch divine!

I was at peace, and drank your beams
As they were life to me
And revelled in my changeful dreams
Like petrel on the sea.

Thought followed thought—star followed star
Through boundless regions on,

While one sweet influence, near and far,
Thrilled through and proved us one.

Why did the morning rise to break *
So great, so pure a spell,
And scorch with fire the tranquil cheek
Where your cool radiance fell?

Blood-red he rose, and arrow-straight
His fierce beams struck my brow:
The soul of Nature sprang elate,
But mine sank sad and low!

My lids closed down—yet through their veil
I saw him blazing still;
And bathe in gold the misty dale,*
And flash upon the hill.

I turned me to the pillow then
To call back Night, and see
Your worlds of solemn light, again
Throb with my heart and me!

It would not do—the pillow glowed
And glowed both roof and floor,
And birds sang loudly in the wood,
And fresh winds shook the door.

The curtains waved, the wakened flies
Were murmuring round my room,
Imprisoned there, till I should rise
And give them leave to roam.

O Stars and Dreams and Gentle Night;
O Night and Stars return!
And hide me from the hostile light
That does not warm, but burn—

That drains the blood of suffering men;
Drinks tears, instead of dew:
Let me sleep through his blinding reign,
And only wake with you!

G21

STARS

Ah! why, because the dazzling sun
Line 2 Restored our Earth to joy
 17 Why did the morning dawn to break
 27 And steep in gold the misty dale

B39

185.   April 22, 1845

A thousand sounds of happiness,
And only one of real distress,
One hardly uttered groan—
But that has hushed all vocal joy,
Eclipsed the glory of the sky,
And made me think that misery
Rules in our world alone!

About his face the sunshine glows,
And in his hair the south wind blows,
And violet and wild wood-rose
Are sweetly breathing near;
Nothing without suggests dismay,
If he could force his mind away
From tracking farther, day by day,
The desert of Despair.

Too truly agonized to weep,
His eyes are motionless as sleep;
His frequent sighs, long-drawn and deep,

Are anguish to my ear;
And I would soothe—but can I call
The cold corpse from its funeral pall,
And cause a gleam of hope to fall
With my consoling tear?

O Death, so many spirits driven
Through this false world, their all had given
To win the everlasting haven
To sufferers so divine—*
Why didst thou smite the loved, the blest,
The ardent and the happy breast,
That, full of hope,[1] desired not rest,*
And shrank appalled from thine?

At least, since thou wilt not restore,
In mercy, launch one arrow more;
Life's conscious Death it wearies sore,
It tortures worse than thee.
Enough of storms have bowed his head: *
Grant him at last a quiet bed,
Beside his early stricken dead—
Even where he yearns to be!

The Reverend A. B. Nicholls has added the title "Despair" in his transcript of this poem.

B40 and B41

186.   A.E. and R.C.   May 28, 1845

Heavy hangs the raindrop
From the burdened spray;
Heavy broods the damp mist
On uplands far away;

---

[1] The word "life" is written over "hope," or vice versa, in the manuscript.

Heavy looms the dull sky,
Heavy rolls the sea—
And heavy beats the young heart *
Beneath that lonely tree.

Never has a blue streak
Cleft the clouds since morn—
Never has his grim Fate
Smiled since he was born.

Frowning on the infant,
Shadowing childhood's joy,
Guardian angel knows not
That melancholy boy.

Day is passing swiftly
Its sad and sombre prime;
Youth is fast invading *
Sterner manhood's time.*

All the flowers are praying
For sun before they close,
And he prays too, unknowing,*
That sunless human rose!

Blossoms, that the west wind *
Has never wooed to blow,
Scentless are your petals,*
Your dew as cold as snow.*

Soul, where kindred kindness
No early promise woke,
Barren is your beauty *
As weed upon the rock.*

Wither, Brothers, wither,*
You were vainly given—*

Earth reserves no blessing
For the unblessed of Heaven!

187. Child of Delight! with sunbright hair,
　　　And seablue, seadeep eyes;
　　　Spirit of Bliss, what brings thee here,
　　　Beneath these sullen skies?

　　　Thou shouldest live in eternal spring,
　　　Where endless day is never dim;
　　　Why, seraph, has thy erring wing *
　　　Borne thee down to weep with him? *

　　　"Ah, not from heaven am I descended,
　　　And I do not come to mingle tears; *
　　　But sweet is day, though with shadows blended;
　　　And, though clouded, sweet are youthful years.

　　　"I, the image of light and gladness,
　　　Saw and pitied that mournful boy,
　　　And I swore to take his gloomy sadness,*
　　　And give to him my beamy joy.*

　　　"Heavy and dark the night is closing;
　　　Heavy and dark may its biding be:
　　　Better for all from grief reposing,
　　　And better for all who watch like me.

　　　"Guardian angel, he lacks no longer;
　　　Evil fortune he need not fear:
　　　Fate is strong, but Love is stronger;
　　　And more unsleeping than angel's care." *

　　Above the heading to the first of these two poems (Nos. 186–187)
Charlotte Brontë has written "The Two Children," the title which
she gave to the poems when they were first printed in 1850.

H485

THE TWO CHILDREN

Heavy hangs the raindrop
[186.] Line 7 And heavy throbs the young heart
         19 Boyhood sad is merging
         20 In sadder manhood's time
         23 And he prays too—unconscious—
         25 Blossom—that the west wind
         27 Scentless are thy petals,
         28 Thy dew is cold as snow!
         31 Barren is thy beauty,
         32 As weed upon a rock.
         33 Wither—soul and blossom!
         34 You both were vainly given:

H486

Child of delight, with sun-bright hair
[187.] Line 7 Why, Seraph, has thine erring wing
         8 Wafted thee down to weep with him?
       10 Nor do I come to mingle tears
       15 And I vowed—if need were—to share his sadness,
       16 And give to him my sunny joy.

After line 20 a stanza of 4 lines was added by Charlotte Brontë:

"Watch in love by a fevered pillow,
Cooling the fever with pity's balm;
Safe as the petrel on tossing billow,
Safe in mine own soul's golden calm!

Line 24 And *my* love is truer than angel-care.

A30

188.   June 2, 1845

How beautiful the Earth is still
To thee—how full of Happiness;

How little fraught with real ill
Or shadowy phantoms of distress; *

How Spring can bring thee glory yet
And Summer win thee to forget
December's sullen time!
Why dost thou hold the treasure fast
Of youth's delight, when youth is past
10 And thou art near thy prime?

When those who were thy own compeers,
Equal in fortunes and in years,*
Have seen their morning melt in tears,
To dull unlovely day; *
Blest, had they died unproved and young *
Before their hearts were wildly wrung,*
Poor slaves, subdued by passions strong,
A weak and helpless prey!

"Because, I hoped while they enjoyed,
20 And by fulfilment, hope destroyed—
As children hope, with trustful breast,
I waited Bliss and cherished Rest.

"A thoughtful Spirit taught me soon
That we must long till life be done;
That every phase of earthly joy
Will always fade and always cloy—*

"This I foresaw, and would not chase
The fleeting treacheries,
But with firm foot and tranquil face
30 Held backward from the tempting race,
Gazed o'er the sands the waves efface
To the enduring seas—

"There cast my anchor of Desire
Deep in unknown Eternity;
Nor ever let my Spirit tire
With looking for *What is to be.*

"It is Hope's spell that glorifies
Like youth to my maturer eyes
All Nature's million mysteries—
40 The fearful and the fair—

"Hope soothes me in the griefs I know,
She lulls my pain for others' woe
And makes me strong to undergo
What I am born to bear.

"Glad comforter, will I not brave
Unawed the darkness of the grave?
Nay, smile to hear Death's billows rave,
My Guide, sustained by thee? *
The more unjust seems present fate
50 The more my Spirit springs elate *
Strong in thy strength, to anticipate
Rewarding Destiny!

Underneath this poem in the manuscript Charlotte Brontë has written
"Never was better stuff penned."

G56

ANTICIPATION

How beautiful the earth is still
Line 4 Or unreal phantoms of distress
      12 Equals in fortune and in years
      14 To clouded, smileless day
      15 Blest, if they died untried and young
      16 Before their hearts went wandering wrong
      26 Must always fade, and always cloy
      48 Sustained, my guide, by thee
      50 The more my spirit swells elate,

On July 31, 1845, Emily Jane and Anne Brontë opened and read their
"papers" of July 30, 1841 (see page 167), and then wrote further papers

with the intention of opening and reading them three years later. Their references to the Gondals are as follows:

Emily wrote: "Anne and I went our first long journey by ourselves together, leaving home on the 30th of June, Monday, sleeping at York, returning to Keighley Tuesday evening, sleeping there, and walking home on Wednesday morning . . . during our excursion we were Ronald Macalgin, Henry Angora, Juliet Augusteena, Rosabella Esmalden, Ella and Julian Egremont, Catharine Navarre, and Cordelia Fitzaphnold, escaping from the palaces of instruction to join the Royalists who are hard driven at present by the victorious Republicans. The Gondals still flourish bright as ever. I am at present writing a work on the First Wars. Anne has been writing some articles on this, and a book by Henry Sophona. We intend sticking firm by the rascals as long as they delight us, which I am glad to say they do at present."

Anne wrote: "Yesterday was Emily's birthday, and the time when we should have opened our 1841 paper, but by mistake we opened it to-day instead. . . . Emily is engaged in writing the Emperor Julius's Life. She has read some of it, and I want very much to hear the rest. She is writing some poetry, too. I wonder what it is about? I have begun the third volume of "Passages in the Life of an Individual." I wish I had finished it. . . . We have not yet finished our Gondal Chronicles that we began three years and a half ago. . . . The Gondals are at present in a sad state. The Republicans are uppermost, but the Royalists are not quite overcome. The young sovereigns, with their brothers and sisters, are still at the Palace of Instruction. The "Unique Society" (see page 193) above half a year ago, were wrecked on a desert island as they were returning from Gaaldine. They are still there. . . . I wonder how we shall all be, and where and how situated on the thirtieth of July, 1848. . . ."

B42

189.   August, 1845

M.A. WRITTEN ON THE DUNGEON WALL—N.C.

I know that tonight the wind is sighing,*
The soft August wind, over forest and moor;

While I in a grave-like chill am lying
On the damp black flags of my dungeon-floor.

I know that the Harvest Moon is shining:
She neither will wax nor wane for me;
Yet I weary, weary with vain repining,
One gleam of her heaven-bright face to see!

For this constant darkness is wasting the gladness,
Fast wasting the gladness of life away:
It gathers up thoughts akin to madness
That never would cloud the world of day.

I chide with my soul—I bid it cherish
The feelings it lived on when I was free,
But shrinking it murmurs, "Let Memory perish,*
Forget, for thy friends have forgotten thee!" *

Alas, I did think that they were weeping
Such tears as I weep—it is not so!
Their careless young eyes are closed in sleeping;
Their brows are unshadowed, undimmed by woe.

Might I go to their beds, I'd rouse that slumber;
My spirit should startle their rest, and tell
How, hour after hour, I wakefully number
Deep buried from light in my lonely cell!

Yet, let them dream on, though dreary dreaming
Would haunt my pillow if *they* were here,
And *I* were laid warmly under the gleaming
Of that guardian moon and her comrade star.

Better that I, my own fate mourning,
Should pine alone in the prison-gloom,*

Than waken free on the summer morning
And feel they were suffering this awful doom.
M.A.

The Reverend A. B. Nicholls gave the title of "The Captive's Lament"
to this poem in his transcript.

B43

190.   October 9, 1845

JULIAN M. AND A. G. ROCHELLE

Silent is the House—all are laid asleep;
One, alone, looks out o'er the snow wreaths deep;
Watching every cloud, dreading every breeze
That whirls the 'wildering drifts and bends the groaning
    trees.*

Cheerful is the hearth, soft the matted floor;
Not one shivering gust creeps through pane or door;
The little lamp burns straight, its rays shoot strong and far;
I trim it well to be the Wanderer's guiding-star.

Frown, my haughty sire; chide, my angry dame;
10 Set your slaves to spy, threaten me with shame:
But neither sire nor dame, nor prying serf shall know
What angel nightly tracks that waste of winter snow.*

In the dungeon crypts idly did I stray,
Reckless of the lives wasting there away;
"Draw the ponderous bars; open, Warder stern!"
He dare not say me nay—the hinges harshly turn.

"Our guests are darkly lodged," I whispered, gazing through
The vault whose grated eye showed heaven more grey than
    blue.

(This was when glad spring laughed in awaking pride.)
20 "Aye, darkly lodged enough!" returned my sullen guide.

Then, God forgive my youth, forgive my careless tongue!
I scoffed, as the chill chains on the damp flagstones rung;
"Confined in triple walls, art thou so much to fear,
That we must bind thee down and clench thy fetters here?"

The captive raised her face; it was as soft and mild
As sculptured marble saint or slumbering, unweaned child;
It was so soft and mild, it was so sweet and fair,
Pain could not trace a line nor grief a shadow there!

The captive raised her hand and pressed it to her brow:
30 "I have been struck," she said, "and I am suffering now;
Yet these are little worth, your bolts and irons strong;
And were they forged in steel they could not hold me long."

Hoarse laughed the jailor grim: "Shall I be won to hear;
Dost think, fond dreaming wretch, that *I* shall grant thy
    prayer?
Or, better still, wilt melt my master's heart with groans?
Ah, sooner might the sun thaw down these granite stones!

"My master's voice is low, his aspect bland and kind,
But hard as hardest flint the soul that lurks behind;
And I am rough and rude, yet not more rough to see
40 Than is the hidden ghost which has its home in me! *

About her lips there played a smile of almost scorn:
"My friend," she gently said, "you have not heard me mourn;
When you my parents' lives—*my* lost life, can restore,*
Then may I weep and sue—but *never,* Friend, before!"

Her head sank on her hands; its fair curls swept the ground;
The dungeon seemed to swim in strange confusion round—

"Is she so near to death?" I murmured, half aloud,
And, kneeling, parted back the floating golden cloud.

Alas, how former days upon my heart were borne;
50 How memory mirrored then the prisoner's joyous morn:
Too blithe, too loving child, too warmly, wildly gay!
Was that the wintry close of thy celestial May?

She knew me and she sighed, "Lord Julian, can it be,
Of all my playmates, you alone remember me?
Nay, start not at my words, unless you deem it shame
To own, from conquered foe, a once familiar name.

"I cannot wonder now at ought the world will do,
And insult and contempt I lightly brook from you,
Since those, who vowed away their souls to win my love,
60 Around this living grave like utter strangers move!

"Nor has one voice been raised to plead that I might die,
Not buried under earth but in the open sky;
By ball or speedy knife or headsman's skilful blow—
A quick and welcome pang instead of lingering woe!

"Yet, tell them, Julian, all, I am not doomed to wear *
Year after year in gloom and desolate despair;
A messenger of Hope comes every night to me,
And offers, for short life, eternal liberty.

He comes with western winds, with evening's wandering
     airs,
70 With that clear dusk of heaven that brings the thickest stars;
Winds take a pensive tone, and stars a tender fire,
And visions rise and change which kill me with desire—*

"Desire for nothing known in my maturer years
When joy grew mad with awe at counting future tears;
When, if my spirit's sky was full of flashes warm,
I knew not whence they came, from sun or thunderstorm;

Julian M. and A.G. Rochelle ─

The Signal Light

Silent is the House - all are laid asleep;
One, alone, looks out o'er the snow-wreaths deep;
Watching every cloud, dreading every breeze
That whirls the wildering drift and bends the groaning trees.

Cheerful is the hearth, soft the matted floor
Not one shivering gust creeps through pane or door
The little lamp burns straight, its rays shoot strong and far
I trim it well to be the Wanderer's guiding star ─

Frown my haughty sire, chide my angry dame;)
Set your slaves to spy, threaten me with shame;
But neither sire nor dame, nor prying serf shall know
What angel nightly tracks that waste of winter snow ─

In the dungeon crypts idly did I stray
Reckless of the lives wasting there away;
"Draw the ponderous bars, open Warder stern"
He dare not say me nay, the hinges harshly turn.

"Our guests are darkly lodged" I whispered gazing through
The vault whose grated eye showed heaven more grey than blue;
(This was when glad Spring laughed in awaking pride,)
"Aye, darkly lodged enough!" returned my sullen guide.

Then, God forgive my youth, forgive my careless tongue!
I scoffed as the chill chains on the damp flagstones rung;
"Confined in triple walls, art thou so much to fear,
"That we must bind thee down and clench thy fetters here?"

The captive raised her face, it was as soft and mild
As sculptured marble saint or slumbering, unweaned child
It was so soft and mild, it was so sweet and fair
Pain could not trace a line nor guilt a shadow there!

The captive raised her hand and pressed it to her brow
"I have been struck, she said, and I am suffering now
"Yet these are little worms, your bolts and irons strong
"And were they forged in steel they could not hold me long"

Hoarse laughed the jailor grim, "Shall I be won to hear
"Dost think, fond dreaming wretch that I shall guard thy prayer?
"Or better still, wilt melt my master's heart with groans
"Ah! sooner might the sun thaw down these granite stones!

"My master's voice is low, his aspect bland and kind
"But hard as hardest flint the soul that lurks behind;
"And I am rough and rude, yet, not more rough to see
"Than is the hidden ghost that has its home in me!"

About her lips there played a smile of almost scorn
"My friend, she gently said, you have not heard me mourn
"When you, my parents lives - my lost life can restore
"Then may I weep and sue, but, never, friend before!"

"But first a hush of peace, a soundless calm descends;
The struggle of distress and fierce impatience ends;
Mute music soothes my breast—unuttered harmony
80 That I could never dream till earth was lost to me.

"Then dawns the Invisible, the Unseen its truth reveals;
My outward sense is gone, my inward essence feels—
Its wings are almost free, its home, its harbour found;
Measuring the gulf it stoops and dares the final bound!

"Oh, dreadful is the check—intense the agony
When the ear begins to hear and the eye begins to see;
When the pulse begins to throb, the brain to think again,
The soul to feel the flesh and the flesh to feel the chain!

"Yet I would lose no sting, would wish no torture less;
90 The more that anguish racks the earlier it will bless;
And robed in fires of Hell, or bright with heavenly shine,
If it but herald Death, the vision is divine."

She ceased to speak, and I, unanswering, watched her there,
Not daring now to touch one lock of silken hair—
As I had knelt in scorn, on the dank floor I knelt still,*
My fingers in the links of that iron hard and chill.

I heard, and yet heard not, the surly keeper growl;
I saw, yet did not see, the flagstone damp and foul.
The keeper, to and fro, paced by the bolted door
100 And shivered as he walked and, as he shivered, swore.

While my cheek glowed in flame, I marked that he did rave
Of air that froze his blood, and moisture like the grave—
"We have been two hours good!" he muttered peevishly;
Then, loosing off his belt the rusty dungeon key,

He said, "You may be pleased, Lord Julian, still to stay,
But duty will not let me linger here all day;

If I might go, I'd leave this badge of mine with you,
Not doubting that you'd prove a jailor stern and true."

I took the proffered charge; the captive's drooping lid
110 Beneath its shady lash a sudden lightning hid:
Earth's hope was not so dead, heaven's home was not so dear;
I read it in that flash of longing quelled by fear.

Then like a tender child whose hand did just enfold,
Safe in its eager grasp, a bird it wept to hold,
When pierced with one wild glance from the troubled hazel
        eye,
It gushes into tears and lets its treasure fly,

Thus ruth and selfish love together striving tore
The heart all newly taught to pity and adore;
If I should break the chain, I felt my bird would go;
120 Yet I must break the chain or seal the prisoner's woe.

Short strife, what rest could soothe—what peace could visit
        me
While she lay pining there for Death to set her free?
"Rochelle, the dungeons teem with foes to gorge our hate—
Thou art too young to die by such a bitter fate!"

With hurried blow on blow, I struck the fetters through,
Regardless how that deed my after hours might rue.
Oh, I was over-blest by the warm unasked embrace—
By the smile of grateful joy that lit her angel face!

And I was over-blest—aye, more than I could dream
130 When, faint, she turned aside from noon's unwonted beam;
When though the cage was wide—the heaven around it
        lay—
Its pinion would not waft my wounded dove away.

Through thirteen anxious weeks of terror-blent delight
I guarded her by day and guarded her by night,
While foes were prowling near and Death gazed greedily
And only Hope remained a faithful friend to me.

Then oft with taunting smile I heard my kindred tell
"How Julian loved his hearth and sheltering roof-tree well;
How the trumpet's voice might call, the battle-standard
   wave,
140 But Julian had no heart to fill a patriot's grave."

And I, who am so quick to answer sneer with sneer;
So ready to condemn, to scorn, a coward's fear,
I held my peace like one whose conscience keeps him dumb,
And saw my kinsmen go—and lingered still at home.

Another hand than mine my rightful banner held
And gathered my renown on Freedom's crimson field;
Yet I had no desire the glorious prize to gain—
It needed braver nerve to face the world's disdain.

And by the patient strength that could that world defy,
150 By suffering, with calm mind, contempt and calumny;
By never-doubting love, unswerving constancy,
Rochelle, I earned at last an equal love from thee!

Under the heading to this poem in the manuscript Charlotte Brontë
has written "The Signal Light."

Lines 13 to 44 and 65 to 92 were printed in *Poems by Currer, Ellis, and
Acton Bell,* 1846, with four additional lines at the end, under the title
"The Prisoner. A Fragment."

Lines 1 to 12 were printed, with 8 additional lines by Charlotte Brontë,
in 1850, under the title of "The Visionary."

The remaining lines, 45 to 64 and 93 to 152, have not previously been
printed in an edition of the poems of Emily Jane Brontë, but see note on
page 35.

G76

THE PRISONER

A Fragment

The "Fragment" commences at line 13:

In the dungeon-crypts idly did I stray
Line 40 Than is the hidden ghost that has its home in me
   43 When you my kindred's lives, *my* lost life, can restore
   65 "Still, let my tyrants know, I am not doomed to wear
   72 And visions rise and change that kill me with desire

After line 92, the "Fragment" ends with the following verse:

She ceased to speak, and we, unanswering turned to go—
We had no further power to work the captive woe;
Her cheek, her gleaming eye, declared that man had given
A sentence unapproved, and overruled by Heaven.

H487

THE VISIONARY

Silent is the house: all are laid asleep
Line 4 That whirls the wildering drift, and bends the groaning trees
   12 What angel nightly tracks that waste of frozen snow

After line 12, the poem ends with 8 lines added by Charlotte Brontë:

What I love shall come like visitant of air,
Safe in secret power from lurking human snare;
Who loves me, no word of mine shall e'er betray,
Though for faith unstained my life must forfeit pay.

Burn, then, little lamp; glimmer straight and clear—
Hush! a rustling wing stirs, methinks, the air:
He for whom I wait, thus ever comes to me;
Strange Power! I trust thy might; trust thou my constancy.

A31

191. Jan. 2, 1846

No coward soul is mine
No trembler in the world's storm-troubled sphere
I see Heaven's glories shine
And Faith shines equal arming me from Fear

O God within my breast
Almighty ever-present Deity
Life, that in me hast rest
As I Undying Life, have power in Thee

Vain are the thousand creeds
That move men's hearts, unutterably vain,
Worthless as withered weeds
Or idlest froth amid the boundless main

To waken doubt in one
Holding so fast by thy infinity
So surely anchored on
The steadfast rock of Immortality

With wide-embracing love
Thy spirit animates eternal years
Pervades and broods above,
Changes, sustains, dissolves, creates and rears

Though Earth and moon were gone
And suns and universes ceased to be
And thou wert left alone
Every Existence would exist in thee

There is not room for Death
Nor atom that his might could render void

Since thou art Being and Breath
And what thou art may never be destroyed.

H489

The following are the last lines my sister Emily ever wrote. (*Note by Charlotte Brontë*)

       No coward soul is mine
Line 7 Life—that in me has rest,
    14 Holding so fast by thine infinity;
    21 Though earth and man were gone,
    23 And Thou were left alone,
    27 Thou—THOU art Being and Breath,
    28 And what THOU art may never be destroyed.

B44

192.   14 September, 1846

Why ask to know the date—the clime?
More than mere words they cannot be:
Men knelt to God and worshipped crime,
And crushed the helpless, even as we.

But they had learnt, from length of strife
Of civil war and anarchy,
To laugh at death and look on life
With somewhat lighter sympathy.

It was the autumn of the year,
10 The time to labouring peasants dear;
Week after week, from noon to noon,
September shone as bright as June—
Still, never hand a sickle held;
The crops were garnered in the field—
Trod out and ground by horses' feet
While every ear was milky sweet;

And kneaded on the threshing-floor
With mire of tears and human gore.
Some said they thought that heaven's pure rain
20 Would hardly bless those fields again:
Not so—the all-benignant skies
Rebuked that fear of famished eyes—
July passed on with showers and dew,
And August glowed in showerless blue;
No harvest time could be more fair
Had harvest fruits but ripened there.

And I confess that hate of rest,
And thirst for things abandoned now,
Had weaned me from my country's breast
30 And brought me to that land of woe.

Enthusiast—in a name delighting,
My alien sword I drew to free
One race, beneath two standards, fighting
For Loyalty and Liberty—

When kindred strive—God help the weak!
A brother's ruth 'tis vain to seek:
At first, it hurt my chivalry
To join them in their cruelty;
But I grew hard—I learnt to wear
40 An iron front to terror's prayer;
I learnt to turn my ears away
From torture's groans, as well as they.
By force I learnt—What power had I
To say the conquered should not die?
What heart, one trembling foe to save
When hundreds daily filled the grave?
Yet, there *were* faces that could move
A moment's flash of human love;
And there were fates that made me feel
50 I was not, to the centre, steel—

I've often witnessed wise men fear
To meet distress which they foresaw;
And seeming cowards nobly bear *
A doom that thrilled the brave with awe.

Strange proofs I've seen, how hearts could hide
Their secret with a life-long pride,
And then reveal it as they died—
Strange courage, and strange weakness too,
In that last hour when most are true,
60 And timid natures strangely nerved
To deeds from which the desperate swerved.
These I may tell; but, leave them now:
Go with me where my thoughts would go;
Now all to-day and all last night
I've had one scene before my sight—

Wood-shadowed dales, a harvest moon
Unclouded in its glorious noon;
A solemn landscape wide and still;
A red fire on a distant hill—
70 A line of fires, and deep below
Another dusker, drearier glow—
Charred beams, and lime, and blackened stones
Self-piled in cairns o'er burning bones,
And lurid flames that licked the wood,
Then quenched their glare in pools of blood.

But yester-eve—No! never care;
Let street and suburb smoulder there—
Smoke-hidden in the winding glen
They lay too far to vex my ken.

80 Four score shot down—all veterans strong;
One prisoner spared—their leader—young,
And he within his house was laid
Wounded and weak and nearly dead.

We gave him life against his will,
For he entreated us to kill—
But statue-like we saw his tears—
And harshly [1] fell our captain's sneers! *

"Now, heaven forbid!" with scorn he said,
"That noble gore our hands should shed
90 Like common blood—retain thy breath,
Or scheme if thou canst purchase death.
When men are poor we sometimes hear
And pitying grant that dastard prayer;
When men are rich we make them buy
The pleasant privilege to die.
O, we have castles reared for kings,
Embattled towers and buttressed wings
Thrice three feet thick and guarded well
With chain and bolt and sentinel!
100 We build our despots' dwellings sure
Knowing they love to live secure—
And our respect for royalty
Extends to thy estate and thee!"

The suppliant groaned; his moistened eye
Swam wild and dim with agony.
The gentle blood could ill sustain
Degrading taunts, unhonoured pain.

Bold had he shown himself to lead;
Eager to smite and proud to bleed;
110 A man amid the battle's storm:
An infant in the after calm.

Beyond the town his mansion stood
Girt round with pasture-land and wood;
And there our wounded soldiers lying
Enjoyed the ease of wealth in dying.

[1] Or "coldly."

For him, no mortal more than he
Had softened life with luxury;
And truly did our priest declare
"Of good things he had had his share."

120 We lodged him in an empty place,
The full moon beaming on his face
Through shivered glass and ruins, made
Where shell and ball the fiercest played.

I watched his ghastly couch beside
Regardless if he lived or died—
Nay, muttering curses on the breast
Whose ceaseless moans denied me rest.

'Twas hard, I know, 'twas harsh to say
"Hell snatch thy worthless soul away!"
130 But then 'twas hard my lids to keep
Through the long night [1] estranged from sleep.
Captive and keeper both outworn
Each in his misery yearned for morn,
Even though returning morn should bring
Intenser toil and suffering.

Slow, slow it came! Our dreary room
Grew drearier with departing gloom;
Yet as the west wind warmly blew
I felt my pulses bound anew,
140 And turned to him—Nor breeze, nor ray
Revived that mould of shattered clay.
Scarce conscious of his pain he lay—
Scarce conscious that my hands removed
The glittering toys his lightness loved—
The jewelled rings and locket fair
Where rival curls of silken hair
Sable and brown revealed to me
A tale of doubtful constancy.

[1] Or "night following night."

"Forsake the world without regret,"
150 I murmured in contemptuous tone;
"The world poor wretch will soon forget
Thy noble name when thou art gone!
Happy, if years of slothful shame
Could perish like a noble name—
If God did no account require
And being with breathing might expire!"
And words of such contempt I said,
Harsh insults o'er a dying bed,
Which as they darken memory now
160 Disturb my pulse and flush my brow.
I know that Justice holds in store
Reprisals for those days of gore;
Not for the blood but for the sin
Of stifling mercy's voice within.

The blood spilt gives no pang at all;
It is my conscience haunting me,
Telling how oft my lips shed gall
On many a thing too weak to be,
Even in thought, my enemy; *
170 And whispering ever, when I pray,
"God will repay—God will repay!"

He does repay and soon and well
The deeds that turn his earth to hell,
The wrongs that aim a venomed dart
Through nature at the Eternal Heart.
Surely my cruel tongue was cursed
I know my prisoner heard me speak
A transient gleam of feeling burst
And wandered o'er his haggard cheek
180 And from his quivering lids there stole
A look to melt a demon's soul
A silent prayer more powerful far
Than any breathed petitions are

Pleading in mortal agony
To mercy's Source but not to me.
Now I recall that glance and groan
And wring my hands in vain distress;
Then I was adamantine stone
Nor felt one touch of tenderness.

190 My plunder ta'en I left him there
Without one breath of morning air
To struggle with his last despair,
Regardless of the 'wildered cry
Which wailed for death, yea wailed to die.*
I left him there unwatched, alone,
And eager sought the court below
Where o'er a trough of chiselled stone
An ice cold well did gurgling flow.
The water in its basin shed
200 A stranger tinge of fiery red.
I drank and scarcely marked the hue;
My food was dyed with crimson too.*
As I went out, a ragged child *
With wasted cheek and ringlets wild,
A shape of fear and misery,
Raised up her helpless hands to me *
And begged her father's face to see.*
I spurned the piteous wretch away
"Thy father's face is lifeless clay *
210 As thine mayst be ere fall of day *
Unless the truth be quickly told—
Where they have hid thy father's gold."
Yet in the intervals of pain
He heard my taunts and moaned again
And mocking moans did I reply
And asked him why he would not die
In noble agony—uncomplaining.*
Was it not foul disgrace and shame
To thus disgrace his ancient name?

220 Just then a comrade hurried in
    "Alas," he cried, "sin genders sin
    For every soldier slain they've sworn
    To hang up five to-morrow morn.
    They've ta'en of stranglers sixty-three,
    Full thirty from one company,
    And all my father's family;
    And comrade thou hadst only one—
    They've ta'en thy all, thy little son."
    Down at my captive's feet I fell
230 I had no option in despair
    "As thou wouldst save thy soul from hell
    My heart's own darling bid them spare
    Or human hate and hate divine
    Blight every orphan flower of thine."
    He raised his head—from death beguiled,
    He wakened up—he almost smiled
    "I lost last night my only child
    Twice in my arms twice on my knee
    You stabbed my child and laughed at me
240 And so," with choking voice he said
    "I trust in God I hope she's dead
    Yet not to thee, not even to thee
    Would I return such misery.
    Such is that fearful grief I know *
    I will not cause thee equal woe *
    Write that they harm no infant there
    Write that it is my latest prayer."
    I wrote—he signed—and thus did save
    My treasure from the gory grave
250 And O my soul longed wildly then
    To give his saviour life again.
    But heedless of my gratitude
    The silent corpse before me lay
    And still methinks in gloomy mood
    I see it fresh as yesterday
    The sad face raised imploringly *

To mercy's God and not to me.
I could not rescue him; his child
I found alive, and tended well
260 But she was full of anguish wild *
And hated me like we hate hell *
And weary with her savage woe
One moonless night I let her go.

This poem was left in an incomplete state by the author. Lines 1 to 148 contain comparatively few alterations, and were probably copied from an earlier draft, but from line 149 onwards the alterations and cancellations are very numerous and much of the script is almost unreadable. Some of the printed words are partly conjectural.

Lines 149 to 156 and 172 to 189 are cancelled by lines drawn across them in the manuscript. A few almost illegible trial lines and parts of lines have been disregarded.

In line 224 "stranglers" may have been written in mistake for "stragglers."

Lines 1 to 8, 27 to 54, and 76 to 263 are now printed for the first time in an edition of the poems, but see note on page 35.

B45

193.   May 13, 1848

Why ask to know what date, what clime?
There dwelt our own humanity,
Power-worshippers from earliest time,
Foot-kissers of triumphant crime *
Crushers of helpless misery,
Crushing down Justice, honouring Wrong:
If that be feeble, this be strong.

Shedders of blood, shedders of tears:
Self-cursers avid of distress; *
Yet mocking heaven with senseless prayers
For mercy on the merciless.

It was the autumn of the year
When grain grows yellow in the ear;
Day after day, from noon to noon,
The August sun blazed bright as June.*

But we with unregarding eyes
Saw panting earth and glowing skies;
No hand the reaper's sickle held,
Nor bound the ripe sheaves in the field.

Our corn was garnered months before,
Threshed out and kneaded-up with gore; *
Ground when the ears were milky sweet
With furious toil of hoofs and feet;
I, doubly cursed on foreign sod,
Fought neither for my home nor God.

CHARLOTTE BRONTË

The following lines, hitherto printed as the work of Emily Jane Brontë, are in the later handwriting (print style) of Charlotte Brontë. They appear to have been written on the day, or an anniversary of the day, when the remains of Emily Jane Brontë were laid beneath the aisle of Haworth Church:

E21

Dec. 23

Not many years but long enough to see
No fo[e] can deal such deadly misery
As the dear friend untimely called away
And still the more beloved, the greater still
Must be the aching void the withering chill
Of each dark night and dim beclouded day

Along the left side of the scrap of paper containing the verse is written "O that word never."

WHO WAS THE AUTHOR
OF THIS POEM?

In 1850 Charlotte Brontë published from her sister Emily's manuscripts "Selections from Poems by Ellis Bell." Though these "selections"
were eighteen in number, only seventeen have been found among
Emily's manuscripts. The remaining poem, the original of which does
not appear, savors more strongly of Charlotte than Emily, seeming to
express Charlotte's thoughts about her sister, rather than Emily's own
thoughts. Since the purpose of Charlotte's publication was to help bring
the public to a better understanding of Emily's work, it would have been
in keeping with the editorial liberties she took in other connections to
offer such an interpretation of her sister in the guise of Emily's own
words.

H489

Stanzas

Often rebuked, yet always back returning
 　　To those first feelings that were born with me,
And leaving busy chase of wealth and learning
 　　For idle dreams of things which cannot be:

To-day, I will seek not the shadowy region;
 　　Its unsustaining vastness waxes drear;
And visions rising, legion after legion,
 　　Bring the unreal world too strangely near.

I'll walk, but not in old heroic traces,
 　　And not in paths of high morality,
And not among the half-distinguished faces,
 　　The clouded forms of long-past history.

I'll walk where my own nature would be leading:
    It vexes me to choose another guide:
Where the gray flocks in ferny glens are feeding;
    Where the wild wind blows on the mountain side.

What have those lonely mountains worth revealing?
    More glory and more grief than I can tell:
The earth that wakes *one* human heart to feeling
    Can centre both the worlds of Heaven and Hell.

INDEX OF FIRST LINES

The letters and figures in the first column indicate the sources from which the text of the poems has been derived (See pp. 24–26). The references in the last column are to pages of the text, not to poem numbers.